Promoting National Foreign Policy

How do smaller member states promote their interests in EU foreign policy and external relations?

EU membership can be seen to affect member states' foreign policy in two ways, either by restricting national policies or empowering states in a challenging global environment. There is a general agreement, however, that the member states, especially smaller ones, have to engage actively in policy-making in order to promote their particular interest.

This cross-policy comparison of the behaviour of Czech Republic's representatives in the Council and the methods they use to influence the decision-making applies categorization from lobbying literature to analyse the behaviour of the member state's representatives and contributes to two strands of scholarship on European Union politics – decision-making in the EU and Europeanization. The book maps the methods of interest promotion that can be used by a member state and analyses the differences in interest promotion across external policy areas.

Tomáš Weiss is Head of the Department of European Studies at the Faculty of Social Sciences, Charles University in Prague, Czech Republic. In his teaching and research, he focuses on EU foreign and security policy, transatlantic relations, and the impact of EU membership on the member states, particularly the Central European countries. He has published in various peer-reviewed journals, including *Cooperation and Conflict, Armed Forces & Society, Geopolitics*, and *Perspectives*. He is the author of a book on Czech security policy published with Charles University Press in 2014, and of a number of book chapters in Czech and English, including with Routledge. He has taken part in numerous international and national research projects. Between 2014 and 2015, he was an external (honorary) advisor to the Ministry of Foreign Affairs of the Czech Republic.

Promoting National Priorities in EU Foreign Policy

The Czech Republic's Foreign Policy in the EU

Tomáš Weiss

Routledge
Taylor & Francis Group

LONDON AND NEW YORK

First published 2017 by Routledge

2 Park Square, Milton Park, Abingdon, Oxon OX14 4RN
605 Third Avenue, New York, NY 10017

Routledge is an imprint of the Taylor & Francis Group, an informa business

First issued in paperback 2021

Copyright © 2017 Tomáš Weiss

The right of Tomáš Weiss to be identified as author of this work has been asserted by him in accordance with sections 77 and 78 of the Copyright, Designs and Patents Act 1988.

All rights reserved. No part of this book may be reprinted or reproduced or utilised in any form or by any electronic, mechanical, or other means, now known or hereafter invented, including photocopying and recording, or in any information storage or retrieval system, without permission in writing from the publishers.

Notice:
Product or corporate names may be trademarks or registered trademarks, and are used only for identification and explanation without
intent to infringe.

Publisher's Note

The publisher has gone to great lengths to ensure the quality of this reprint but points out that some imperfections in the original copies may be apparent.

British Library Cataloguing in Publication Data
A catalogue record for this book is available from the British Library

Library of Congress Cataloguing in Publication Data
Names: Weiss, Tomáš, 1980– author.
Title: Promoting national priorities in EU foreign policy: the Czech Republic's foreign policy in the EU / Tomáš Weiss.
Description: Abingdon, Oxon; New York, NY: Routledge, 2017. | Series: Routledge advances in European politics |
Includes bibliographical references and index.
Identifiers: LCCN 2016038498| ISBN 9781138215528 (hardback) | ISBN 9781315443843 (e-book)
Subjects: LCSH: Czech Republic–Foreign relations–1993– | European Union–Czech Republic. | National interest–Czech Republic.
Classification: LCC JZ1584.W45 2017 | DDC 327.4371–dc23
LC record available at https://lccn.loc.gov/2016038498

ISBN: 978-1-138-21552-8 (hbk)
ISBN: 978-1-03-217928-5 (pbk)
DOI: 10.4324/9781315443843

Typeset in Times New Roman
by Out of House Publishing

Contents

List of figures vii
List of tables viii
List of abbreviations ix
Acknowledgements xii

1 Introduction 1

   Identifying the gap in the literature 2
   Advocating individual interests 8
   Research questions and the focus of the book 13
   Research method and the selection of cases 15
   Structure of the book 18

2 The Czech Republic in the EU: from a new member state to a member state 20

   Czech foreign policy interests 22
   Czech coordination of European affairs 24
   Coordination of external policies 28
   Representation of Czech interests in external relations 31

3 Perceptions of Czech representatives in the Council of their work 34

   Collection period, response rate, and structure of respondents 40
   Experience of Czech diplomats posted in Brussels 41
   Methods and tools for Czech interest promotion 43
   Human resources and their exploitation 57
   Summary of the chapter's findings and partial conclusions 58

4 External trade: reforming the Generalised System of Preferences 62

   Motivation and proposal for change 63
   Negotiation framework and results 64

vi *Contents*

    Czech interest and engagement in EU external trade 66
    Formulation of the Czech negotiation position 67
    Czech activity during the negotiations 68
    Evaluation of the Czech engagement 70

5 European Neighbourhood Policy: introducing the more-for-more principle to the European Neighbourhood Instrument   73

    Motivation and proposal for change 74
    Negotiation framework and results 76
    Czech interest and engagement in the European Neighbourhood Policy 78
    Formulation of the Czech negotiation position 80
    Czech activity during the negotiations 81
    Evaluation of the Czech engagement 82

6 Democracy and human rights: implementing the recommendations of EU Election Observation Missions   85

    Motivation and proposal for change 87
    Negotiation framework and results 88
    Czech interest and engagement in EU Election Observation Missions 90
    Formulation of the Czech negotiation position 91
    Czech activity during the negotiations 92
    Evaluation of the Czech engagement 94

7 Common Security and Defence Policy: extending the mandate for EUMM Georgia in 2014   97

    Motivation and proposal for change 98
    Negotiation framework and results 99
    Czech interest and engagement in the CSDP 100
    Formulation of the Czech negotiation position 102
    Czech activity during the negotiations 103
    Evaluation of the Czech engagement 104

8 Conclusions   107

    Main findings of the book 108
    Relevance for the academic literature 112
    What does the Czech case say about other member states? 114
    Opportunities for further research 115

    List of interviews   117
    Bibliography   120
    Index   136

Figures

3.1	Number of respondents according to the year they finished their tenure in Brussels	42
3.2	Number of respondents according to the level of the working group and policy area	42
3.3	Average number of methods "never" used according to year	44
3.4	Use of interest promotion methods in individual policy areas	46
3.5	Use of interest promotion methods over time	46
3.6	Use of interest promotion methods at different negotiation levels	48
3.7	Use of interest promotion methods in European Neighbourhood Policy	48
3.8	Perceived value of tools for promoting or blocking a proposal	50
3.9	Perceived value of tools for promoting a proposal at different levels	51
3.10	Perceived value of tools for blocking a proposal at different levels	53
3.11	Correlation between the Czech representatives' activity and what they perceive as important for promoting and blocking agendas	54
3.12	Factors' importance for promoting Czech influence (average)	55
3.13	Factors' importance for promoting Czech influence according to policy area (average)	56

Tables

1.1	Overview of case studies	17
3.1	Questionnaire	35
3.2	Previous experience in diplomacy or related area of public administration I (in years)	43
3.3	Previous experience in diplomacy or related area of public administration II (in years)	43
3.4	Distribution of methods of interest promotion into three groups	45
3.5	Correlation between which factors are considered important and which factors hinder Czech performance	57

Abbreviations

CARIFORUM	Caribbean Forum
CBM	confidence building measure
CFSP	Common Foreign and Security Policy
CivCom	Committee for Civilian Aspects of Crisis Management
CMPD	Crisis Management and Planning Directorate
COAFR	Africa Working Party
COASI	Asia-Oceania Working Party
COEST	Working Party on Eastern Europe and Central Asia
COHOM	Working Party on Human Rights
COLAC	Working Party on Latin America and the Caribbean
COREPER	Committee of Permanent Representatives
COREU	European Correspondence (Correspondance Européenne)
COTRA	Working Party on Transatlantic Relations
CPCC	Civilian Planning and Conduct Capability
CSDP	Common Security and Defence Policy
DAP	Database of European Policies
DEMAS	Association for Democracy Assistance and Human Rights
DEVE	Committee on Development
DG	Directorate-General
DG DEVCO	Directorate-General for International Cooperation and Development
DG ELARG	Directorate-General Enlargement
DG TRADE	Directorate-General for Trade
EaP	Eastern Partnership
EaPIC	Eastern Partnership Integration and Cooperation
EBA	Everything but Arms
EEAS	European External Action Service
EIDHR	European Instrument for Democracy and Human Rights
ENI	European Neighbourhood Instrument

ENP	European Neighbourhood Policy
ENPI	European Neighbourhood and Partnership Instrument
EODS	Election Observation and Democratic Support
EOM	Election Observation Mission
EP	European Parliament
EU	European Union
EUBAM	European Union Border Assistance Mission
EULEX	European Union Rule of Law Mission
EUMM	European Union Monitoring Mission
EUSR	European Union Special Representative
EUTM	European Union Training Mission
FORS	Czech Forum for Development Cooperation
GATT	General Agreement on Tariffs and Trade
GSP	Generalised System of Preferences
HoM	Head of Mission
HR	human rights
INTA	Committee on International Trade
IPA	Instrument of Pre-accession Assistance
LDC	least developed country
MaMa	Mashreq/Maghreb Working Party
MEP	Member of the European Parliament
MFA	Ministry of Foreign Affairs
MFN	most favoured nation
MIT	Ministry of Industry and Trade
NATO	North Atlantic Treaty Organization
NGO	non-governmental organization
ODIHR	Office for Democratic Institutions and Human Rights
OECD	Organization for Economic Co-operation and Development
OLP	Ordinary Legislative Procedure
OSCE	Organization for Security and Co-operation in Europe
PMG	Politico-Military Group
PSC	Political and Security Committee
pVEU	European Union Committee at the working level
RKS	Sectorial Coordination Group (Resortní koordinační skupina)
SPRING	Support to Partnership, Reform and Inclusive Growth
TEU	Treaty on the European Union
TPC	Trade Policy Committee
UfM	Union for Mediterranean
UK	United Kingdom

UN	United Nations
VEU	European Union Committee (Výbor pro Evropskou unii)
vVEU	European Union Committee at the governmental level
WP	Working Party
WTO	World Trade Organization

Acknowledgements

This book would not have been possible without support from numerous institutions and individuals. My gratitude belongs to the Czech Science Foundation in the first place for its financial support through its postdoc grant scheme, grant number P408-12-P493. I would also like to thank the Faculty of Social Sciences, Charles University and its Institute of International Studies for granting me a sabbatical that allowed me to concentrate on research without interruption for a few months, and to Zuzana Kasáková who covered for me during my absence. Partial results have already been published by the *New Perspectives* journal (2016) and I am grateful to the journal's editor, Benjamin Tallis, for his permission to use parts of the text in this book.

Various individuals have commented on parts of this text or the ideas that formed the basis of the project. Without any particular order, and giving up hope that I have mentioned everybody, I would like to thank Fabienne Bossuyt, Jan Karlas, Lucia Najšlová, Karolina Pomorska, Ivo Šlosarčík, participants of the IMS research seminar, and audiences and fellow panellists at the UACES conventions in Leeds and Bilbao, as well as the EUIA IV and V conferences in Brussels. Explicit gratitude belongs to Petr Soukup for his help with and advice on the survey. Also I would like to acknowledge Pamela Cotte for her superb editing and proofreading work as well as her substantial comments on the text.

This research would not have been possible if people working for Czech and European institutions and various think tanks and NGOs had not been ready to talk to me about their jobs and their perceptions of EU decision-making. This is particularly true for those who found the time to fill in the survey. I am grateful for their time and insight, while recognizing that all omissions and errors remain mine. A special thank you belongs to Aranka Slabová, Livia Tereniová, David Král, and Jan Kára, who helped me enormously in putting together a list of Czech officials who had served at the Czech permanent representation to the EU and were responsible for the relevant working groups and committees.

Above all, my gratitude goes to my family, which has supported me and encouraged me to take up, conduct, and finish this project.

1 Introduction

This book asks how a small and new European Union member state pursues its interests in EU foreign policy-making. It aims at contributing to two strands of academic debate. First, it adds to the extensive literature on decision-making in the EU by mapping the informal methods that a member state uses to shape the resulting compromise in the Council and beyond. It builds on rational choice institutionalism, which presumes that member states' policies are influenced by international institutions in general and, in particular, that they use these institutions to strengthen their position vis-à-vis other actors in the negotiations. In other words, the member states come to the negotiation table with predefined interests and priorities. The ways and strategies used to persuade the partners at the table and promote their particular preferences in the final policy are, however, tailored to the institutional setting. This may include specific behaviour, negotiation tactics, or image-building, but may also result in giving up on some interests in order to gain elsewhere.

Second, it contributes to the literature on Europeanization, more specifically to the literature on the Europeanization of member states' foreign policy. It compares a member state's strategies in various foreign/external policy areas and asks to what extent the different institutional and procedural frameworks lead the member state's representatives to choose distinct methods and tools to promote their position. As such, this research focuses on the Europeanization of national foreign policy structures and strategies, rather than national foreign policy content.

In mapping the methods of one member state's negotiators, this research draws from the literature on advocacy and lobbying. Despite significant differences, the position of the EU member states in the Council, in particular the smaller member states, resembles in many respects the situation of advocates of private interests. The scholarship on lobbying offers valuable insight into the policy-making process from the perspective of actors who are disadvantaged in terms of power and resources, access to information and access to decision-makers, which largely captures the situation of small member states in the Council.

2   Introduction

This chapter introduces the two strands of literature that this book builds on and contributes to. It shows that the main puzzle of this book directly follows from the two debates, neither of which offers a satisfactory answer. The literature on lobbying is introduced to help guide the research and structure the methods that a member state may use into a coherent framework. Furthermore, the research questions and hypotheses are laid out, the choice of case studies explained, and the structure of the book introduced.

Identifying the gap in the literature

European foreign policy-making and small member states

Much of the EU decision-making literature has focused on the policy areas where the Council decides by qualified majority with full participation of the other institutions. Scholars have studied the distribution of power among the institutions (Costello and Thomson, 2013; Häge, 2010) and, particularly, states in the Council, identifying the combinations that allow for qualified majorities and blocking minorities, and the shifts caused by every new enlargement and revision of the treaties (Beisbart et al., 2005; Carrubba and Volden, 2001; Hosli, 1996; Hosli et al., 2011; Mattila, 2004; Nurmi and Hosli, 2003; Selck, 2006). In these accounts, the states and the institutions are, to a large extent, unitary actors that maximize their gains in the negotiations. The states are affected by the institutions in their decisions on when and how to pursue their interests, but they enter the negotiations with predefined interests and behave rationally to 'maximise utility' (Veen, 2011: 4), hence the label 'rational choice institutionalism' (Hall and Taylor, 1996).

EU foreign and security policy has, in this tradition, been understood as a domain where the member states' concerns about influence and sovereignty have precluded the introduction of majority rule, resulting in intergovernmental decision-making. In such a setting, the Council and the European Council are the dominant institutional actors that decide unanimously over new policies and their implementation. As a result, the member states retain full control over the policy, because their (at least tacit) approval is necessary for any decision to take place (cf. White, 2001: 97). In rational choice institutionalism, the bigger and richer member states are more influential than the smaller and poorer in EU decision-making because they have more power to persuade their negotiation partners with threats, side offers, or issue linkages (cf. Hayes-Renshaw and Wallace, 2006: 252; Hix and Høyland, 2011; Pedersen, 1998; Thomson, 2011: 212ff.). Given the requirements of unanimity, however, the bigger member states are more powerful in shaping the final decision, but the smaller ones still have the power to block if they are unhappy with the negotiation results. This leads inevitably to a least common denominator policy, or, on much-contested issues, no policy at all.

In contrast, accounts drawing from constructivist arguments have highlighted different aspects of EU policy-making. In particular, they study changes in the positions of individual actors as well as adjustments of national policies under the influence of the Brussels milieu through socialization (Beyers and Trondal, 2004; Checkel, 2005; Juncos and Pomorska, 2006; Lewis, 2005). From this perspective, the informal rules that shape Brussels negotiations (cf. Heisenberg, 2005) as well as forms of negotiation other than size and power-related bargaining, such as arguing (Reinhard, 2012; Risse, 2000) and problem-solving (Elgström and Jönsson, 2000), become important for success. Consequently, size and economic power, while still relevant, are not necessarily key factors for achieving a member state's objectives. The experience of negotiators (Meerts, 1997; Tallberg, 2008: 698), length of EU membership (Wallace, 2005: 38; cf. Lewis, 2008), or specific expertise relevant for the issue at hand (Haverland and Liefferink, 2012; van Keulen, 2006: 22) may be more important. As a result, as Golub (2012) suggests, many smaller member states are indeed surprisingly successful in Council negotiations. From this point of view, foreign and security policy-making are not qualitatively different from other policy areas. The mere fact that the policy is discussed at the EU level brings about the socialization of actors and allows for smaller member states with sufficient expertise and experienced negotiators to have a significant imprint on the resulting policy.

While not questioning the underlying assumptions as the constructivist literature has done, recent scholarship tends to problematize the intergovernmental account of EU foreign policy-making. It argues that small member states cannot rely on unanimous decision-making as much as intergovernmentalists used to believe.[1] The negotiation dynamics in practice differ from what the treaty text would imply (cf. Sjursen, 2011; M Smith, 2004; Stetter, 2004). Unlike the big states, smaller countries use the veto parsimoniously and substantiate it with significant national interest (Heisenberg, 2005: 77; Tallberg, 2008: 691). This means that in order to secure favourable negotiation results small member states need to employ other negotiation methods beyond the mere threat of veto.

Both accounts of EU policy-making agree that the small member states need to work hard to shape EU foreign policy decisions. They may differ on how much the small member states can achieve: for constructivists they can match the influence of big countries; for intergovernmentalists they struggle to have any influence at all. The emphasis on the states' activity in the negotiations is, nevertheless, common to both.

There is, however, very limited knowledge about the ways through which the small member states pursue their foreign policy objectives in EU negotiations. So far, the literature on small member states has dealt primarily with what they strive for (Thorhallsson and Wivel, 2006; Wivel, 2005) and whether they have any influence in the Council at all (Jakobsen, 2009; Kronsell, 2002; Romsloe, 2004). The few studies that have addressed the member states' practices of interest promotion focused on either single case studies (cf. Arter, 2000) or selected channels of influence, such as norm advocacy or holding the Council presidency (cf. Björkdahl, 2008; Bunse, 2009).

There are two notable attempts to classify small member states' activities in EU decision-making. First, Skander Nasra (2011) offered a set of factors to assess small member states' ability to exert influence and applied it to the Belgian attempts to shape EU policy towards the Democratic Republic of Congo, showing that small member states are able to steer EU policy effectively in specific circumstances. For Nasra, four factors are important in this respect: commitment to specific EU policies; formation of self-organizing informal groups or networks; politically relevant resources in these networks; and ability to justify, explain and persuade other actors.

Second, in an extensive combination of quantitative and qualitative research, Diana Panke (2010b, 2010c, 2010a, 2011) studied the small member states' strategies in three selected policy areas and measured their activities and success. Panke grouped the member states' activities into two types: capacity-building, which should compensate for a lack of domestic capacities and expertise, such as collecting additional information from the Commission or the presidency and specialization on selected dossiers; and shaping, which covers all efforts to influence the actual negotiations, such as arguing, bargaining, problem-solving, lobbying, and coalition-building. However, Panke's research compared small member states' activities in agricultural, economic, and environmental policies, i.e. "first pillar" only. Although we might expect that some of her findings will hold for foreign policy, the different decision-making mode and distinct involvement of other EU institutions, such as the limited role of the European Parliament and specific position of the European External Action Service (EEAS), may require different behaviour from the member states.

Europeanization and foreign policy

The concept of Europeanization became widely used in the academic literature around the turn of century (Olsen, 2002: 922). It has taken a while, however, to define what exactly the term means and how it differs from other concepts used in European integration research. Individual scholars have used the label Europeanization for various phenomena that often did not relate to each other and this concept stretching hampered mutual understanding (Radaelli, 2003: 27; cf. Sartori, 1970: 1034). In his review of the current debate, for example, Olsen (2002) distinguished five different uses of the term in scholarly literature: changes in EU external boundaries; developing institutions at the EU level; central penetration of national systems of governance; exporting forms of political organization; and a political unification project. Europeanization became a modern concept utilizable in many research directions, but it could not focus the scholarly debate around a single phenomenon to be studied and understood.

Olsen's list also suggested that Europeanization in its broadest understanding had a potential overlap with a number of other concepts from the very beginning. The creation of new institutions at the EU level has, for example, been described as supranationalism (Stone Sweet and Sandholtz, 1998; Stone Sweet et al., 2001) and political unification explained by federalism or neofunctionalism. Multi-level governance, in turn, analyses the shift in decision-making from the national to subnational and supranational levels (Hooghe and Marks, 2001; Marks et al., 1996). The broad application of the concept has blurred the fact that Europeanization should not be considered a theory, but a 'phenomenon which a range of theoretical approaches have sought to explain' (Bulmer, 2007: 47). Correspondingly, some authors analysing the same issue, i.e. the relationship between the European and national levels, have managed to avoid the term Europeanization altogether (Kassim et al., 2000; Wessels et al., 2003).

Even today, various applications of Europeanization can be found in EU studies and related disciplines. As historians, for example, Conway and Patel (2010) conceptualize Europeanization as the series of social and economic processes that have been connected to the label "European" in history, meaning not only EU integration, but also mutual delimitation and conflict. In this respect, their use of the term does not only concern Europe and it does not have any significant relation to the EU at all. Nevertheless, most scholars have accepted that Europeanization means the mutual influence between the European and the national levels in the first place.

The concept of Europeanization consists of three distinct, though mutually interrelated, directions of influence: besides the European influence on the domestic level (*downloading*) there also is the domestic influence on the EU level (*uploading*) and the influence by the member states on one another (*cross-loading*) (Howell, 2009). Today, it is mainly applied to analyse the impact of European integration on domestic institutions and policies only (Axt et al., 2007; Bache and Marshall, 2004; Börzel and Risse, 2000; Bulmer and Radaelli, 2004; Faist and Ette, 2007; Graziano and Vink, 2007; Hughes et al., 2005; Ladrech, 2010; Larsen, 2005; Lenschow, 2006; Wong, 2006). Some scholars, however, include all the dimensions, particularly national interest promotion at the EU level, into their analysis because they see them as closely related to the domestic adaptation processes (Bomberg and Peterson, 2000; Börzel, 2002, 2003; Bulmer et al., 2007; Tulmets, 2009). Analysis of the domestic institutions as an independent variable is important because they co-determine the exact integration impact on the particular member state (Bache and Marshall, 2004: 1–2; Fontana, 2011; Héritier, 2001; Mastenbroek and Kaeding, 2006; Radaelli and Pasquier, 2007: 39; Risse et al., 2001).

Interest promotion at the EU level (*uploading*) remains on the margin of the mainstream Europeanization research.[2] This is despite the accepted fact that the capability to pursue national interests in the EU is a function of the ability of national institutions to adjust to Brussels' written and unwritten norms (cf. Lewis, 2008), and that the Europeanization pressures on the national level depend on the lack of fit between national and European policies (Börzel, 2002; Börzel and Risse, 2000). Adaptation to integration and pursuing one's own interests is, thus, mutually constitutive. The academic debate does acknowledge this – in fact, it is considered one of the biggest methodological problems of the whole Europeanization concept where the dependent and independent variables are not easily recognizable (cf. Caporaso, 2007). It is, however, ignored deliberately and the research focuses on one direction only, the EU's impact on the national level.

In the beginning, the Europeanization research focused on communitarian policies, such as environmental policy (cf. Börzel, 2002). Foreign policy was considered a unique policy area where the adaptation to European integration remains less probable, the impact less visible, and also difficult to analyse (de Flers and Müller, 2012; Major, 2005; Miskimmon and Paterson, 2003). Unlike in the communitarian policies, the member states retained much greater control over the developments with the elevated role of the EU Council and the unanimous decision-making. As a result, a mismatch between the national and the European levels was considered nearly impossible. Should a member state disagree with a policy, there was always the option to veto.

Increasingly, however, it became clear that the situation with foreign policy was more complicated. Some studies revealed that Europeanization is effective beyond the original research framework that focused on the adaptation of member states to their obligations resulting from the Community policies and the activity of EU institutions; the influence of EU integration was possible to trace in countries that were not members of the European Union (Ozel, 2013; Schimmelfennig and Sedelmeier, 2007). Moreover, adaptation to EU membership was observed in policies that had not been fully constituted at the EU level, such as defence policy (Irondelle, 2003). Other scholars hinted at the fact that member states adjust their foreign policy-making to European integration (ME Smith, 2004). There was, therefore, no reason not to study foreign policy through Europeanization lenses (Moumoutzis, 2011). In fact, it is rather remarkable that the relevance of Europeanization for foreign policy used to be disputed. Some of the path-leading studies quoted in most of the later research did not at least suggest that national adaption required enforcement of EU rules. Knill and Lehmkuhl (2002), for example, defined three Europeanization mechanisms that they related to three types of EU policy-making. One of them expected a change of opinions and expectations at the national level following simply framing of an issue at the level of the EU. The weakly institutionalized common foreign and security policy fits into this model.

Literature on the Europeanization of foreign policy is, however, still scarce and only a handful of authors focus on this field. At the same time, the existing research suffers from the same shortcomings as the bulk of Europeanization literature: namely, the concentration on changes at the national level and the lack of linkage between downloading and uploading. One group of papers focuses on the adjustment of national institutions to European integration, particularly of the foreign ministries. Pomorska (2007), for instance, has shown using the example of the Polish Ministry of Foreign Affairs how the new member states had to learn to work with the abundant intra-EU CFSP communication after accession. A second, more numerous group of authors deals with the adjustment of national foreign policy content (Larsen, 2005; Miskimmon, 2007; Palosaari, 2011; Raimundo, 2013; Torreblanca, 2001; Wong, 2006; Wong and Hill, 2011).

The effect of European integration varies across policy areas because it depends on the mode of common policy-making. Prescriptive or positive integration with enforceable regulation has a different impact than negative integration or discursive integration, which is restricted to framing a topic at the EU level (Faist and Ette, 2007; Knill and Lehmkuhl, 2002). The intensity of integration plays a role too, because well-established and far-reaching policies at the EU level tend to engage a bigger number of national actors and shape more domestic policies. Similarly, policy areas with a strong role of EU institutions induce different national behaviour than policy areas where the EU institutions play a marginal part. This suggests that the impact of integration will also vary in various forms of EU external relations, which cover a broad range of policies from foreign trade, which is a supranational policy, to CSDP where the role of EU institutions is the weakest.

At the same time, Europeanization does not necessarily mean unification. Although the pressure from the European level may be similar in all member states, the impact is shaped by national institutions, procedures and traditions (Major, 2005; Ozel, 2013; Radaelli and Pasquier, 2007; Zubek, 2008). In parallel, the different domestic contexts may produce various modes of uploading efforts with diverse results.

To sum up, the issue of member states' activities in uploading their preferences into and shaping EU foreign policy is grossly under-researched, but highly relevant for our understanding of the decision-making process in the EU and the role played by small states. There is agreement on the fact that the small member states can shape EU foreign policy in the decision-making literature, but little knowledge about how they do it. For its part, the Europeanization literature suggests that member states' foreign policy, both in content and in institutions, is affected by European integration, and that this impact in turn influences the ways in which the member states engage in EU foreign policy-making, but again fails to study how the uploading of national preferences looks and varies from one policy or country to another.

This book addresses exactly this gap in the literature by studying the methods that a single member state uses to shape EU external policies across several policy areas. In doing so, it works on the assumption that the role of member states' representatives in EU Council negotiations is similar to the role of advocates for private/individual interests – lobbyists (Hayes-Renshaw, 2009: 81).[3] Like lobbyists they have their position/interests defined in advance by the constituency they represent (the national governments), they need to persuade other actors that their view is relevant, and often they must react to initiatives that other actors put forward unexpectedly. Naturally, there are significant differences between the representatives of states and of private interests during EU decision-making. Most notably, the state representatives are members of the Council and Council working groups and, as such, they have access to the formal negotiations and they co-decide on the final text. In foreign policy, moreover, they even possess a veto over the final decision.

This does not, however, hold fully for the small member states. They cannot always rely on the veto, as argued above. Even though they are members of the decision-making bodies, much of the actual decision-making has moved from the formal meetings (cf. Edwards, 2006: 13–14; Hertz and Leuffen, 2011; Juncos and Pomorska, 2007: 7). Instead of debating the substance of the matter in the format of 28 member states, the bulk of the agenda is pre-negotiated during informal consultations among smaller groups of actors. Moreover, the Lisbon Treaty has established the EEAS to coordinate EU foreign policy-making, chair most Council working groups dealing with foreign policy and set their agendas. Scholars have pointed out that the permanent chairs in foreign policy potentially diminish the influence of small member states, because the EEAS would be inclined to work with the big countries more closely (cf. Gaspers, 2008: 26). Due to these specific constraints affecting small EU member states, inquiry into the methods through which small member states attempt to influence EU foreign policy-making could draw on lobbying literature and apply classifications that have been developed to study private interests.

Advocating individual interests

Private interest representation is a complex issue and existing research has shown that lobbying in the EU differs depending on issue and policy area (Mahoney, 2008: 6; cf. Pedler and Schendelen, 1994). There is a multitude of factors that determine what lobbying strategy should be chosen. These may range from the institutional characteristics (such as type of decision-making procedure and number of involved actors) to issue characteristics (such as salience, degree of change sought, power of the status quo, and issue history) to the lobbyist's motivation (namely, whether the change should be initiated or prevented) (cf. Baumgartner et al., 2009: 113ff.; Mahoney, 2008: 35–36; Zetter, 2011: 29).

In the private interest representation literature, there are two main groups of interest promotion activities: inside advocacy and outside advocacy (Mahoney, 2008: 34; Zetter, 2011: 37). They may also be labelled as "access" and "voice" (Bouwen and Mccown, 2007: 423) and depend on the interaction of the advocate with the decision-maker. Outside advocacy relies on communication with the decision-maker through the public. The advocate voices his or her opinions in public statements, such as opinion papers, reports, and op-eds. In the broadest form of outside advocacy, grassroots or even general public mobilization may take place in order to influence the decision-maker (Baumgartner et al., 2009: 150ff.). Inside lobbying, on the other hand, is based on direct contact with the policy-maker. The advocate attempts to influence him or her in person by highlighting options, risks, and opportunities at personal meetings, testifying at public hearings, or even by drafting legislative language. The initiative may stem from the advocate who asks for a meeting, mails position papers and policy briefs, or actively participates in a seminar or a consultation. In terms of efficiency, however, the advocate's ultimate goal is to become a recognized stakeholder who is invited to consultations by the policy-makers themselves (Greenwood, 2011: 23).

Another possible classification reflects the rationale of the advocate's activity. Lobbyists are important contributors to the decision-making system. They provide specialist information to the generalist policy-makers (Klüver, 2012: 491). From the perspective of the lobbyist, however, introduction of new regulation may be both a blessing and a curse, an opportunity and a threat (Zetter, 2011: 29). Therefore, the representatives of individual interests need to monitor the developments in the policy sphere and establish an 'early warning system' (Joos, 2011: 43) capable of scanning for issues on the agenda that may have impact on their interests, establish contacts with insiders, i.e. identify the 'access points' (Watts, 2007: 45), and prepare detailed key player analyses. In addition, lobbying can also take the form of political crisis management (Joos, 2011: 43) in case the policy debate heads in an inconvenient direction.

There is broad agreement among scholars studying private interest representation that lobbyists are first and foremost sources of information for the policy-makers (Klüver, 2012). Consequently, some authors have even equated the lobbyists' ability to process information with their influence (cf. Chalmers, 2011). This is too much of a simplification though. Interest groups do not only bring in practical experience and specialized knowledge, but they are also necessary for correct implementation of the final decisions – either by implementing themselves or by informing the broader population (Watts, 2007: 46).

But how can an advocate persuade the policy-maker that his or her view should prevail? That depends, in part, on whether the policy-maker in question is a directly elected or a non-elected official. Whereas directly elected politicians are largely driven by the re-election motive and open to constituent mobilization threats, non-elected officials need to be won by the quality of argumentation and importance of the information and expertise to be shared (Mahoney, 2008: 3–4). Unlike traditional forms of persuasion, such as seduction, negotiation, authority and coercion (cf. van Schendelen, 2010: 45–47), lobbying relies mostly on non-violent argumentation. Advocacy may be based on arguments related to commonly shared goals, referencing positively viewed concepts that everybody would support. Alternatively, it may be anchored in technical expertise supporting the advocate's view. It may be more implementation-oriented, focusing on either the economic impacts or the broader feasibility and workability of a proposal. Alternatively, the argument may be grounded in the notion of fairness and acceptability by the constituency (Mahoney, 2008: 83–84). Often, the argumentation will be adjusted according to the lobbied person – a technical argument for a bureaucrat, a political one for a politician.

The importance of argumentation does not mean that other, more traditional methods cannot be used. In particular, teaming up with other actors raises visibility and occurs both in long-term alliances and in ad hoc coalitions (cf. Pijnenburg, 1998; Hula, 1999). Sometimes, bargaining takes place between the policy-makers and interest groups, perhaps the most institutionalized forum being trialogues between policy-makers, employers, and employees (cf. Treib and Falkner, 2009). And finally, the context is of utmost importance, so changing the context by reframing the issue at hand may alter the set of involved actors, arguments, and consequently the results (Baumgartner and Mahoney, 2008).

Choosing the right lobbying strategy is important, but every strategy will fail unless it is backed by a clear definition of the advocate's objective and internal cohesion. Most academic studies of lobbying focus on the interaction between the advocate and the policy-maker and take the clear definition of the objective for granted. Practitioners' accounts, however, highlight the utmost necessity to 'manage the home front' first (van Schendelen, 2010: 199ff.; cf. Zetter, 2011). Most interest groups are composed of various actors with differing views and priorities and also there are usually several advocates arguing on behalf of the same actors. It is therefore crucial that they pursue a common objective, although their strategies might be tailored to the situation and lobbied subject.

In economic policies, the EU is described as an elite pluralist system because of the Commission's efforts to engage business interests and its bias towards them (Coen, 2007: 335). In fact, as Coen argues (2007: 336), EU lobbying is characterized by the institutions reaching out to and sometimes even funding private and public interest representation, rather than being aggressively lobbied by them. This is in line with Baumgartner et al.'s general finding (2009: 110) that lobbyists are surprisingly often reactive, rather than proactive. Hence, it is all the more important to become one of the few that are invited to express their opinion by the Commission. Even more so, because in the EU's multi-level system of governance, the early phases of the policy process, namely the agenda-setting phase and early policy formulation phase, have been recognized as decisive in influencing the shape of the final decision (Quittkat and Kotzian, 2011: 405).

To sum up the lessons from the lobbying literature, a successful advocate needs to have good knowledge of the policy area, including the key access points, positions of individual actors, and timely information about the agenda. A wide spectrum of strategies can be employed depending on the dossier at hand – from public campaigning to targeted meetings with selected individuals – with a plethora of tactics ranging from political and technical argumentation to bargaining to changing the context. In particular, however, the advocate needs to be recognized as a relevant actor for the particular dossier by the policy-makers themselves. Such recognition guarantees an invitation to preparatory meetings and consultations, and sometimes even gives a chance to co-draft legislative language. Obtaining this "insider" position increases the chances to participate in the negotiations from the very beginning and to shape the original proposal, which is the most efficient way of influencing the final decision.

Three types of strategies can thus be broadly identified. First, there are *strategies that focus on a particular dossier* under negotiation. These strategies are generally reactive. The lobbyists approach the decision-makers during the negotiation process and they try to influence their positions and to create winning or blocking coalitions. Depending on the issue at stake and the specific setting, these strategies may include arguing, bargaining, reframing an issue as well as approaching key decision-makers and providing them with political or expertise-based arguments.

Second, there are less focused activities that aim at gathering information and providing *early warning*. This type of strategy helps lobbyists to engage in negotiations from the early phases, thus increasing the chance for greater influence. Early warning may be obtained by various means and from various sources. In the EU context, informal contacts in EU institutions provide a useful source of information about the future consultations and proposals. Participation and organization of social events serve as fora where future plans and views can be informally discussed among stakeholders. Consultations with non-governmental representatives, such as social partners, think tanks and NGOs, feed in different perspectives and points of analysis.

Third and most importantly, there are activities that do not necessarily touch upon a concrete issue, but increase the lobbyists' profile in the respective policy area or topic and help them *obtain insider status*. Insider status can be both objectively and subjectively induced. If the lobbyists are stakeholders at the same time who implement the planned policy in practice or who manage key resources, such as hardware, know-how, or information that are indispensable for successful implementation, they are insiders for objective reasons. For example, social partners can be considered objective insiders in labour legislation because they are the direct addressees and it is useful for a policy-maker to consult with social partners on any planned legislation to ensure its smooth implementation. Lobbyists can, however, push their way into the insiders' circles even without such objective reasons simply through consistency and articulation. When considering legislation on access to data and transparency in the public sphere, for example, Transparency International, an NGO, is often invited to give testimony and advice. There are multiple reasons to include such actors. First, they dispose of expertise and knowledge, including good and bad practice that is useful in drafting the legislation and that could be considered an "objective" asset. In addition, however, these actors are the first to criticize in public a decision that they consider wrong. Involving them in the decision-making effectively disqualifies them as critics.

The lobbyists can actively create both objective and subjective reasons for obtaining insider status. Investing in assets that are necessary to implement a successful policy, obtaining relevant market share, building knowledge and skills, and collecting information are all steps that increase the profile of the lobbyists and help them become recognized as important stakeholders. Similarly, consistent specialization and public activity in a selected policy area or even on a particular topic may elevate the recognition of the lobbyists and earn them an invitation to the inner circle of relevant actors.

Relevance for EU foreign policy-making

May any of this be relevant for EU foreign policy-making? The short answer is, it may. Although EU foreign policy or even broader external policy is in many ways specific, the patterns and tools identified in the lobbying literature exist in EU foreign policy-making too. There is a defined set of actors and decision-makers, comprising both elected and non-elected individuals. The access to various phases of decision-making may be restricted to some stakeholders, including member states' representatives.

First, it is necessary to recognize that the term EU foreign policy or even broader EU external relations covers a number of policy areas with different sets of actors, different decision-making procedures, and different objectives, such as common security and defence policy, neighbourhood policy, enlargement policy, and foreign trade. As a result, lobbying in EU foreign policy must be flexible and adjust to the specific context using a broad range of tools and methods. At the same time, given the interconnection among these policy areas, there is significant potential to reframe an issue and shift the decision-making from one area to another or to bundle several dossiers together.

Second, the policy-makers in EU foreign policy and external relations are both elected politicians and non-elected officials, but the latter group dominates. The preparatory phases, including the drafting and agenda setting, are led by the European External Action Service and the European Commission. The actual decision-making phase is dominated by the Council, which is, of course, composed of politicians, i.e. ministers from the member states. The majority of the dossiers are, however, concluded at lower levels and reach the ministers as point A (without debate) only, which means that it is the national officials who negotiate the compromises most of the time (cf. Hayes-Renshaw and Wallace, 2006). The role of the European Parliament, although growing and occasionally crucial, is still rather limited in foreign policy and the institution lacks the administrative capacity to become a stronger actor (cf. Cameron, 2012: 240). In general, therefore, expertise and technical argumentation should be more important for a foreign policy lobbyist than political argumentation, even though from time to time the latter may be useful or even necessary.

Third, a clearly defined objective is required for coordinated and successful lobbying in foreign policy as in any other policy area. Given the complexity of most issues and the ease with which a dossier may cross borders between individual foreign policy areas, however, the internal coordination and definition of common goals may become a particularly difficult task. The academic literature and policy discourse are full of examples that link (foreign policy) objectives that are not easily reconciled, such as trade and human rights, democracy and stability, and security and liberty (cf. Hollis, 2012; Meunier and Nicolaïdis, 2006; Balzacq and Carrera, 2006).

Research questions and the focus of the book

This research joins the current trend in EU decision-making scholarship that strives to bridge the rationalist and idealist (or sociological) approaches, which is also visible in the Europeanization literature (Börzel and Risse, 2003; Drulák, 2010; Lewis, 2005; Palosaari, 2011; Saurugger, 2013; ME Smith, 2004). It builds on the assumption that there are two levels of analysis that can be separated from each other for research purposes, although they are necessarily interlinked in practice. The first level of analysis is the overall and long-term impact of European integration on the member state. From this perspective, the socialization of member states' representatives (and ultimately their publics) leads to changes in behaviour (type I socialization) and even to changes in interests and identities (type II socialization) (Checkel, 2005). The second level of analysis addresses the individual cases of negotiation in which the representatives of the member states engage. In these cases, the negotiators enter the process with pre-identified interests and rationally maximize utility during the negotiations. In this respect, it is to be expected that the states use various methods to push through their preferences in the final policy within the limits of what is considered appropriate in the negotiating environment.

By focusing on the latter level, the maximization of utility in individual cases, this research aims to fulfil two objectives. First, it studies and categorizes the methods that a member state's (the Czech Republic) representatives employ to influence the resulting policy and uncovers the factors that contribute to the particular choice of strategy. Second, by comparing the application of the methods across several foreign policy areas and over a period of ten years, it tests hypotheses that derive from the first level of analysis. It takes a bird's-eye view of a member state and situates the individual cases into the broader context of the change induced by EU membership. The general research question can thus be formulated in the following way: *How does the Czech Republic, as a smaller EU member state with limited membership experience, pursue its interests in EU foreign policy-making?*

The hypotheses that form the departure point of this research derive from both the Europeanization and lobbying scholarship. The Europeanization scholarship suggests that member states change through EU membership over time. Their representatives learn how to navigate in the EU, find out who and what is important, how to obtain relevant information, and how to formulate their opinions in a manner that is acceptable for their partners. Simply, they learn to pull the strings to promote their national interests more actively and effectively. This learning naturally takes place at a personal level since all officials serving in Brussels know the EU environment better towards the end of their posting period than at the beginning. It occurs, however, at the national level as well and we can expect a state as such to know the Brussels environment better the longer it is an EU member. This is due to two parallel processes that ensure that the results of the personal learning are not lost. In the first process, the incoming officials are put on the job by the incumbents who introduce them to their contacts and advise them on what to do and what to avoid. As a result, every subsequent official can be expected to start with better knowledge of the environment than his or her predecessor. In the second process, the acquired knowledge is translated into adjustments of the national processes and structures. The officials rotate from Brussels back to the ministries and bring back the awareness of where the system may be inefficient. At the same time, the ministry itself gains more experience with the EU agenda with every new dossier and is able to evaluate the effectiveness of its strategies. The first working hypothesis can therefore be formulated as follows:[4]

H1: The number of different methods that the member states' negotiators employ while pursuing national interests in the EU increases over time.

Not all activities and strategies are equally effective. It has been shown that three broad groups of strategies can be identified: those focused on a specific dossier, early warning strategies, and strategies for obtaining insider status. They vary in effectiveness, because generally speaking there is more chance of success when early warning or even insider status support specific negotiations. They also vary in sophistication, because whereas everybody is able to take part in Council negotiations and bargain there, only experienced member states know how to gather timely information or even become insiders where required. In order to be able to employ the more sophisticated strategies, the member states and their representatives need to know the Brussels environment well, have a clear understanding of their own priorities and preferences, and have a well-designed domestic coordination system. Most of these points do not appear overnight with the country's EU membership. They rather evolve in time along with the growing experience with EU decision-making. Subsequently, the second hypothesis can be formulated as follows:

H2: The efforts of member states' representatives to employ early warning methods and methods for obtaining insider status increase over time.

This learning does not occur homogeneously across all policy areas. In some policy areas the EU agenda is denser than in others; the negotiators meet more often and they address more issues. The role of EU institutions varies across policy areas too and so does the decision-making procedure, which again affects the impact of the integration on the member states. In addition, some policy areas are more salient than others, particularly those dealing with money where the success or failure of negotiators can be directly calculated in terms of gains and losses for the national economy.[5] All these factors push the member states' representatives to be more active and inventive in their national interest promotion. As a result, the third hypothesis can be formulated as follows:

> *H3: The member states' negotiators will be more likely to employ early warning methods and methods for obtaining insider status in policy areas that are more salient and in which the European institutions play a greater role.*

Research method and the selection of cases

This research is based on a cross-policy area and diachronic comparison of a single member state's performance in the EU Council – the Czech Republic. Given that it is the cross-policy analysis which is the focus here, the restriction to a single country is preferable. Focusing on a single member state makes the cross-policy comparison more valid, because the data all stem from a single national system with single decision-making procedures and coordination practices. The variations can therefore be ascribed more reliably to the differences in policy areas. In addition, it allows an actor-oriented analysis of individual cases that is more focused and in-depth.

There are some limitations resulting from the one-country research design. Above all, the generalization of the findings is fairly limited. Each country adjusts differently to the pressures of EU membership depending on its history, administrative structures, and politics, to name but a few factors. As a result, the conclusions drawn from the Czech case cannot be fully applicable even to other "new" member states, not to mention countries that have joined the EU at a different point in history and under different structural conditions. The exploration of the Czech case can, nevertheless, lead to hypothesizing about other member states that will need to be tested by future research.

The Czech Republic has been selected for several reasons. First, the Czech Republic has been an EU member for a little over ten years now, which allows for capturing the change during the first years of its membership. This is the period in which the adjustment to the EU environment takes place and the change and variation should be visible. Moreover, the whole period of membership can be covered in the research, because the number of officials representing the country in Council preparatory groups is still rather limited. At the same time, however, it is a period long enough for the adjustment to take place and for the state administration to develop a functioning coordination mechanism and to learn how to pull the strings in Brussels. A factor not unimportant in this respect was the 2009 Czech Council presidency. It is widely acknowledged in the literature that the new member states grasp the finesses of Council negotiations only with their first presidency (Bunse,

2009: 213; Luif, 2006; Panke, 2010c: 813). Last but not least, the author's long-term focus on Czech foreign policy made it possible to benefit from contacts and trust within the Czech administration built in past research projects. Such access is crucial in research focused on the everyday practice of and self-evaluation by stakeholders.

There are four specific policy areas under scrutiny: external trade, European Neighbourhood Policy, democracy and human rights, and Common Security and Defence Policy. All of them can be subsumed under the broader label of foreign policy or external relations. They all vary in decision-making and the involvement of EU institutions. The ordinary legislative procedure is used in external trade with the full participation of the European Commission and the European Parliament. The policy has a direct financial impact on member states' companies and economies and can thus be considered very salient. The European Neighbourhood Policy, for its part, is to a large extent run by the EU institutions, particularly the Commission with important input by the EEAS. It also has a significant financial dimension, although in this case it instead concerns money flowing from the member states (through the EU budget) to the countries in the EU neighbourhood. The policy on democracy and human rights belongs to the CFSP and as such relies on unanimity among the Council members. Yet, there is important input by the Commission and the EEAS, including specific financial resources earmarked for the policy. Lastly, the CSDP remains at the core of the intergovernmental approach in EU foreign policy. Despite the growing role played by the EEAS recently, the decision-making remains firmly in member states' hands both during the policy design and the implementation.

In addition, the four policy areas represent two distinct fields from the perspective of Czech foreign policy priorities (see Chapter 2 for more details). The Czech Republic has participated in foreign trade and CSDP actively, but neither of them has ever been truly crucial from the national perspective, because the bulk of Czech national interests are materialized in the internal market and Czech security is primarily anchored in NATO. The other two areas, ENP (particularly its Eastern dimension) and policy in support of democracy and human rights have belonged among proclaimed Czech priorities. Besides the impact of EU institutions and money, the research can thus also examine how salience in terms of definition of foreign policy priorities impacts the practice of member state representatives in the Council.

The research is based on a combination of a small-scale survey and a comparative case study method. Throughout the book, the frequency and type of employed methods of interest promotion serve as the dependent variables. The length of membership and salience of the policy area constitute, in turn, independent variables. First, a survey of Czech representatives in selected Council working groups and committees aims at confronting the working hypotheses with what methods they have employed and which strategies they consider most useful for their work. Given the size of the N (fewer than 50 officials have represented the Czech Republic in these groups so far), the data serve for preliminary testing and refinement of the working hypotheses, rather than providing a basis for strong testing. The survey helps understand *which* methods are used to promote specific interests in the Council, allowing for comparison between individual policy areas as well as for comparison over time. It covers the four policy areas targeted in this book and the period between the Czech accession to the EU in 2004 and the year 2015 when the survey was conducted.

Second, a qualitative analysis is conducted on four cases, one from each policy area. The empirical material was collected mainly using interviews with participants from the Czech public administration, EU institutions, other member states, and non-state actors where relevant.[6] While it was quite simple to contact the Czech officials engaged in the negotiations, it was relatively more difficult with the representatives of other actors. Often they either did not recall the details of the negotiation (unlike for the Czechs, it was one of many similar dossiers on the agenda) or it was impossible to trace and contact the particular individual who took part in the negotiations due to rotation or transfer to another job. The participants' accounts and interpretations were therefore triangulated with the help of publicly available documents. The case studies help unveil *why* some methods were preferred to others and why the Czech Republic decided to actively engage in that specific negotiation in the first place.

The four policy areas are sufficiently broad to cover a large number of negotiation processes on individual dossiers. The specific dossiers for the case studies were identified by the stakeholders themselves through interviews during the preparatory research phase. They were asked to identify a particular decision in their area of work where the Czech Republic had put the most effort in influencing the final policy. The case studies serve the distinct purpose of analysing the choices and limitations behind Czech interest promotion. The most salient cases with the highest level of activity reveal the most about the Czech practice. If a specific path of interest promotion is not developed in these cases, it implies that the Czechs are not able or willing to employ this type of activity in Council negotiations. Table 1.1 provides an overview of the cases singled out during the interviews.

Table 1.1 Overview of case studies

Policy area	Case study
External trade	Generalised System of Preferences reform in 2012
European Neighbourhood Policy	Introducing the more-for-more principle
Democracy and human rights	Inclusion of support for implementation of election observation missions' recommendations into the EIDHR action plan
Common Security and Defence Policy	Strategic review of the EUMM Georgia in 2013–2014

Structure of the book

The remainder of the book is structured in the following way. First, the Czech Republic's position in the EU is introduced in Chapter 2. The chapter introduces the context of the Czech Republic's EU membership and the structures shaping Czech EU policy. Attention is paid to the Czech priorities in EU foreign policy and the coordination mechanisms employed in preparation for Council negotiations. In Chapter 3, the results of the survey are presented and analysed. The three working hypotheses are directly confronted with the data and additional preliminary findings are drawn from the results. The data sketch a picture of how the Czech Republic promotes its interests in EU foreign policy across policy areas and across time. In the next four chapters, the four case studies are presented, one for each policy area: foreign trade, European Neighbourhood Policy, policy in support of democracy and human rights, and the Common Security and Defence Policy. At the end of each chapter, the Czech activity in the individual negotiation processes is discussed and preliminary conclusions are drawn as to why the Czech Republic behaved in such a manner. Finally, Chapter 8 connects all the bits and pieces together and concludes. It sums up the findings and suggests what they could mean for small states in the EU in general, for the newer small states in particular, and what further research paths they open up.

Notes

1 There is a thriving body of literature on small states based on the realization that the number of small states has increased considerably during the past century (Panke, 2012: 313) and that small states 'today enjoy more international prestige and visibility than at any other time in history' (Hey, 2003: 1). There are many ways to define smallness and the approach has been changing. While objective criteria, such as the geographic, demographic, or economic size of the country, were often used in the past, current research has mainly adopted 'a dynamic definition by considering smallness through its relation with power' (Rickli, 2008: 309), i.e. a relational definition that suggests that states can be small in one relationship but big in another (cf. Baldacchino, 2009; Maass, 2014; Steinmetz and Wivel, 2010; Wivel et al., 2014). This is also true for the research on small states in the EU, where no definition has been considered wholly satisfactory (Archer and Nugent, 2002: 4). Whereas some authors have relied on objective criteria, such as a below-average number of votes in the Council of the EU (Panke, 2010b), others have defined smallness in relational terms (Thorhallsson and Wivel, 2006: 658). This research follows the fuzzier relational definition of smallness and understands small states as those that have their policy options more restricted than others in a given relationship due to more limited resources and capacities. The Czech Republic, whose behaviour is the main focus of this book, can be considered a smaller EU member by this account.
2 Many other streams of scholarship such as liberal intergovernmentalism, to name but one, focus on how member states shape resulting EU policies. The concept of uploading is, however, specific in linking the creation of EU policies directly with the institutional change at the member state level and there is not much research on this specific connection.
3 I use the terms lobbying, advocacy, and private/individual interest representation interchangeably, as is common in the lobbying literature.

4 It remains obvious that the increase over time cannot continue indefinitely. It should be expected in the first years after the accession until the member state learns what is there to learn.
5 The money factor is visible in private interests' involvement in foreign policy and external relations decision-making. Coen (2007) shows, using European Commission data, that there are approximately twice as many interest groups active in "external trade" than in "external relations".
6 Over 50 interviews were conducted – most of them in person in Brussels and Prague or, where a personal meeting was not possible, via telephone and, on one occasion, via email. Within the Czech administration, the group of interviewees partly overlapped with the respondents of the survey, but the interviews focused on the specific cases, not the general perception of the interviewees' work. In most cases, there were several months between the date of the interview and the date of the survey. See the list of interviews at the end of the book.

2 The Czech Republic in the EU

From a new member state to a member state

The Czech Republic became an EU member on 1 May 2004 together with another seven countries of the former Soviet bloc, Cyprus and Malta. The accession crowned the period of intensive preparations for membership that started in the first half of the 1990s. Two major shifts occurred in May 2004, one concerning the administrative contacts between the EU and the Czech Republic and the second relating to the political debate on the EU and foreign policy in general.

Administratively, the Czech Republic was generally prepared for the membership in 2004. After all, the accession negotiations that lasted for almost five years not only put the Czech legal order in line with the acquis, but also acquainted portions of the Czech administration with the EU and EU law. European sections were created at line ministries responsible for coordinating the EU-related agenda. In addition, the Czech representatives had the opportunity to participate in all Council meetings as observers since the signature of the Accession Treaty in December 2002. They could familiarize themselves with the working environment at all Council levels and prepare for what they were supposed to co-create in future (cf. Šlosarčík, 2006).

It would be, however, naive to consider the Czech administration fit for EU membership and fully able to promote Czech interests in the EU right from the beginning. There are well-documented accounts that suggest that new member states have fully grasped the volume of the EU agenda only when becoming full members (cf. Pomorska, 2007). The knowledge of EU affairs was limited to islets of excellence within the public administration: to the EU sections at the individual ministries and the few individuals that actually worked in Brussels or with Brussels directly. The Czech officials thus had to learn as they went along. It was not until the preparations for the 2009 Czech Council presidency that the government ran an extensive educational programme that spread the understanding of EU matters more widely across the Czech public administration (cf. Král et al., 2009). Even then, however, the expertise often flowed away to European institutions or, occasionally, to European politics (several current MEPs elected in the Czech Republic are former officials specialized in EU affairs). The public administration often lost expertise due to unstable rules for employing civil servants in the past, which could result in extensive reshuffling of ministries' staff with every new administration. The Czech Republic introduced a long-expected act on a regulated civil service only in 2015 (fully in force since July 2015).[1] It is to be seen whether the new act will have a stabilizing effect on the civil service and will contribute to better accumulation of knowledge in the public administration.

While the officials were improving their understanding of the EU and other segments of Czech society also underwent the process of Europeanization (Brusenbauch Meislová, 2012; cf. Fiala et al., 2007; Hloušek and Pšeja, 2008; Sedláček, 2010; Zemanová, 2008), the quality of political debate stalled at best. There had never been a comprehensive debate on the EU in the Czech Republic, even before the accession (cf. Vajdová, 2003).[2] EU membership was presented as the culmination of the Czech "return to Europe", a process of coming back to the rightful place among the (West) European democracies from which the country was ripped away by Nazism and communism, a process that had no alternative. EU membership (together with NATO membership) became a Czech foreign policy objective, but there was no debate about the post-accession period and what the long-term foreign policy objectives of the Czech Republic would be when the accession process was completed.

After 2004, foreign policy disappeared from the Czech public debate. It seemed that all foreign policy goals had been accomplished and the Czech politicians lived in a sort of "end of Czech history" that allowed them to focus just on the domestic agenda. Only occasionally did some aspects of foreign affairs become politicized enough to attract the attention of Czech politicians and the Czech media, but even those were used for domestic political gains and did not provoke an in-depth debate on foreign policy content, such as the Czech debate on the third site of the US ballistic missile defence (Hynek and Střítecký, 2010a, 2010b; Přikryl, 2006). This ignorance largely concerned the European Union as well, which enabled the president, Václav Klaus, to monopolize the topic in the public discourse (cf. Řiháčková and von Seydlitz, 2007). The Czech debate on the EU remained oversimplified, relying on vague and often loaded terms, such as 'Euro-realists' and 'Euro-toadies' (Weiss, 2015b).

There are several practical implications of the lack of the public debate. As the EU is not understood well and it conjures up a relatively negative image for Czech voters (European Commission, 2015), very few politicians are ready to connect their career in domestic politics with European issues.[3] The Czech parliament's European committees have traditionally struggled with lack of parliamentary interest (Němec and Kuta, 2015) and ministers have often avoided participation in Council meetings. Although the situation has improved recently and the government has announced that the decline in ministers' Council activity had been reversed, the situation is still dismal in some cases (Government of the Czech Republic, 2015d), which does not serve the Czech interests well.

The government launched a public consultation campaign in the form of a "National Convention on the EU" in 2014 to engage with various segments of civil society in its European policy-making and to raise public awareness of EU matters. In the longer term, higher public awareness could increase the interest among politicians as well. In addition, the current government seems to have largely stabilized the system of coordination of European affairs in the Czech public administration, which was undergoing continuous reform in the past years. This will be addressed in more detail in the following sections, but first the content of Czech foreign policy interests should be briefly introduced.

Czech foreign policy interests

The key to every successful interest promotion activity by a complex organization, such as a member state, is the identification of the interest and coordination of the various actors that represent the organization in negotiations with partners (cf. van Schendelen, 2010: 199ff.; Zetter, 2011). This book is not primarily concerned with the definition of the Czech national interests and the content of Czech policies and positions in EU bodies, which has been addressed elsewhere (Drulák and Braun, 2010; Drulák and Handl, 2010; Drulák and Horký, 2010; Drulák and Střítecký, 2010), but it needs to briefly introduce which areas are important for the Czech Republic. For the analysis presented in the following chapters, it is fundamental to understand the priorities of Czech foreign policy and the policy areas and individual dossiers in which the Czech Republic would be more active than elsewhere.[4]

Foreign policy priorities are traditionally anchored in basic conceptual documents, notably the Concepts of the Czech Republic's Foreign Policy, which are adopted by the Czech government at regular intervals. Further information about Czech foreign policy accents can be taken from the governmental programmes that each government presents to the parliament prior to the vote of confidence. Since 1993, there have been 13 governments each with its own programme and four foreign policy concepts. The first foreign policy concept was drafted in 1999 for the first time since the establishment of an independent Czech Republic (Government of the Czech Republic, 1999; cf. Kotyk, 2000: 56); the subsequent concepts were adopted in 2003, 2011, and 2015 respectively (Government of the Czech Republic, 2003, 2011a, 2015a).

There are several themes that appear in all the concepts and have undergone no or very limited development in time. The first constant is the emphasis on international organizations. The Czech Republic is described as a small state or 'a small country in a global context and a medium-sized country on a European scale' (Government of the Czech Republic, 2015a: 2) and as such, it needs international organizations to promote its interests and secure its well-being. The accent on individual organizations changes dependent on current Czech membership (from the OSCE to NATO to the EU), but the general priority remains stable.

The second constant is the focus on human rights, democracy, and assistance to countries in transition from authoritarian forms of rule, i.e.

transformation cooperation in the Czech terminology (cf. Weiss, 2015a). All the concepts understand human rights and democracy as the 'fundamental values' of its foreign policy (Government of the Czech Republic, 1999). Democracy cannot remain an internal affair of individual countries, but 'the best basis for the successful development of mutual relations' (Government of the Czech Republic, 2003). Given Czech history and the perceived importance of Western support to dissident movements during communism, 'the Czech Republic feels that it is naturally obliged to follow suit in assisting those who strive for freedom and other values referred to above and welcome Czech assistance' (Government of the Czech Republic, 2011a: 5). In 2015, human rights and democracy were not only described as the value basis of Czech foreign policy, but at the same time also became, as part of human dignity, one of its five main objectives (Government of the Czech Republic, 2015a: 4). Furthermore, the Czech Republic aims at actively advocating support for democracy and human rights, which, together with rule of law and freedom, should remain 'the cornerstone of the EU's external action' (Government of the Czech Republic, 2011a: 5).

A third constant concerns security and how it should be provided. While the Czech Republic declares that the best way to ensure international security is through the United Nations, international organizations, and international law, the specific security of the Czech Republic has been closely linked to NATO in all concepts.[5] The Czech Republic understands the transatlantic bond as the 'backbone of the European security system' (Government of the Czech Republic, 2003) and the Alliance's collective defence system as 'the basic pillar' (Government of the Czech Republic, 2011a: 11) and 'primary tool' (Government of the Czech Republic, 2015a: 5) of Czech security policy. In this context, the European security and defence policy is recognized as an important tool, but remains secondary. The Czech Republic supports further development of an active and capable CSDP 'while taking into account its NATO commitments' (Government of the Czech Republic, 2011a: 11).

A fourth constant is the relatively low profile of foreign trade beyond the European internal market, although economic diplomacy and the search for economic opportunities remain present in all documents. The concepts sum it up neatly and unambiguously: 'Territories outside the OECD and EU are also important, although less than 10% of total Czech exports are destined for these countries' (Government of the Czech Republic, 2011a: 11). 'The European Union is and will remain the main platform for the pursuit of our foreign economic interests' (Government of the Czech Republic, 2015a: 7). In the EU Common Commercial Policy, the Czech Republic generally supports further liberalization of world trade within the WTO as well as conclusion of bilateral free trade agreements between the EU and third countries.

Fifth, Czech foreign policy has a very narrow geographical focus, which nevertheless is slowly expanding due to global developments and the need to participate in EU foreign policy. Most attention has always been paid to the immediate neighbours and broader Central Europe. Further, the United

States as the crucial partner in NATO enlargement first and key ally later has traditionally deserved consideration. For similar reasons France and the United Kingdom have always been mentioned explicitly as potential or actual allies and important EU member states. Beyond the EU and NATO members, however, not much loomed large in Czech foreign policy with the exception of Eastern and South-Eastern Europe, where the Czech Republic had traditional ties and interests. In the 1999 and 2003 concepts, for example, all other regions and states of the world were packed into a single chapter 'The Czech Republic and Countries of Asia, Africa, Australia and Latin America' (cf. Government of the Czech Republic, 2003). This worldview confined to the nearest neighbourhood has been partially abandoned since the 2011 concept and other regions have attracted slightly more nuanced treatment. The focus on Eastern and South-Eastern Europe has, however, remained unchanged (see also Weiss, 2015a for more discussion on the position of Eastern Europe in Czech foreign policy). It was not until the 2015 concept that North Africa and the Middle East deserved more attention as the result of 'its mounting instability and unpredictability and by its spiralling number of armed conflicts' (Government of the Czech Republic, 2015a: 17). It still remains part of a subchapter labelled 'Other Territories', together with all world regions beyond the Euro-Atlantic area.

To sum up the priorities relevant for this book, two of the four policy areas cover the proclaimed prerogatives of Czech foreign policy. The policy in support of democracy and human rights is both a basic value and objective for the Czech Republic and the European Neighbourhood Policy covers one of its key geographic regions – Eastern Europe. The other half of the ENP, which focuses on North Africa, is, however, of lesser importance for the Czechs. On the other hand, foreign trade and CSDP are not priorities for the Czech Republic's foreign policy. Even though there is interest in certain types of foreign trade policy and specific developments of the CSDP, the Czechs connect their primary economic interest with the internal market and their security with NATO.

Czech coordination of European affairs

Having briefly introduced what the Czech Republic prioritizes in the foreign policy domain, it is now necessary to describe the main legal and procedural framework in which the positions to be promoted in Brussels are developed. The focus remains on official procedures that bind politicians and civil servants, but where appropriate, the informal aspects of the system are mentioned and the role of non-governmental actors is discussed.

The political level

The logical place to start is the Constitution of the Czech Republic, which delineates competences among the most important actors in the Czech political system. There is a sharing of competences between the president and the government within the executive branch of power. While the president is the head of state (Art. 54) and shall 'represent the State with respect to other countries' (Art. 63), the government is the 'supreme body of executive power' (Art. 67). This has led to some confusion in the past, particularly when the presidents disagreed with the governments on foreign policy content. It could be argued, however, that this confusion has always been merely a result of domestic politics and the relative power of the actors, not the constitution itself. According to constitutional experts, the government is the superior body in terms of running the state and determining policies. In particular, all of the agenda that is not explicitly entrusted to the president is the responsibility of the government. In international relations, in addition, all acts by the president listed in the constitution require co-signature by the prime minister or another member of the government and the government is accountable for such acts (Sládeček et al., 2007: 485, 498). For the EU context this means that the government is responsible for managing the agenda as well as representing the Czech Republic in EU bodies, including the European Council where the prime minister acts on behalf of the state. In principle, however, the country could be represented by the president, as was the case during the Czech Council presidency in 2009 when the president chaired several summits between the EU and third countries.

The so-called 'European amendment' of the constitution enabled a 'transfer of certain powers' to international organizations or institutions (Art. 10a) and also defined the role of the parliament in European affairs. Both chambers of the parliament have the right to be informed 'regularly and in advance' and can 'express their opinions on the decisions' of the international organizations or institutions of which the Czech Republic is a member (Art. 10b). Both the Chamber of Deputies and the Senate have established specialized committees on 'European affairs' and 'EU affairs' respectively.

Within the government, the competences of individual line ministries are set by the 'competence law' (no. 2/1969 Coll.). There was no complex reform of the law after the accession, rather a number of partial amendments were adopted; the European agenda was mentioned in the law only marginally and there was no definition of the coordinating body (Šlosarčík, 2006). As a result, there has been room for competence clashes between some governmental institutions over which should be the coordinating body of Czech EU policy and the responsibility has moved from one institution to another during the past 20 years depending on the political context and functional needs.

Currently, the office of the government coordinates the European agenda in the Czech Republic with significant support provided by the Ministry of Foreign Affairs. The system seems well established now, having survived a change of the government, but this does not mean that it will not change in future, in detail or completely. Until the Czech accession to the EU, the coordination of European affairs was entrusted to the Ministry of Foreign Affairs, with the brief exception of 1998–1999 when a special position of deputy prime minister for European affairs was established. The office of the government gained the upper hand again before the Czech Council presidency, when the position of deputy prime minister for European affairs was re-established and tasked with the coordination of the presidency agenda. After the government fell in the middle of the presidency, the caretaker government retained the European agenda at the governmental level, but this time only at the level of a regular minister for European affairs.

Since 2010, however, the position of a government member responsible for European affairs has been abandoned. Instead, a state secretary for European affairs was appointed at the office of the government (a senior civil servant at the rank of managing director), directly responsible to the prime minister. A rope pulling game continued for a while between the office of the government and the foreign ministry, where another state secretary for European affairs was appointed (double-hatted with the first deputy minister), but it seems to have been decided in favour of the office of the government.[6] In the current administration, the position of state secretary for European affairs does not exist any more at the foreign ministry and the system is clearly centred on the state secretary at the office of the government. At the same time, however, it is mostly the minister of foreign affairs who attends the General Affairs Council meetings, only occasionally substituted by the state secretary.

Administrative structures

The Czech system of coordination of European affairs is generally classified as 'semi-centralized' or 'rather centralized' by experts (Krutílek, 2013; Marek and Baun, 2010). It revolves around the European Union Committee (Výbor pro Evropskou unii; VEU), which is the highest body responsible for Czech EU policy in all policy areas. Similar to the Council structure, the VEU works at several levels from the highest political level, where it comprises the whole government, to specialized working groups at line ministries.

In principle, there are three levels of the Czech coordination system: the governmental level VEU (vládní VEU; vVEU), working level VEU (pracovní VEU; pVEU), and the so-called Sectorial Coordination Groups (Resortní koordinační skupiny; RKS) at every ministry (Government of the Czech Republic, 2014b). The vVEU is chaired by the prime minister and it is composed of all members of the government as regular members and a number of representatives from other state bodies as associated members, including the head of the office of the president, the governor of the Czech National Bank, and the Czech permanent representative to the EU. The foreign minister is the deputy chair of the vVEU. At the working level, the pVEU is nominally also chaired by the prime minister (with the foreign minister as a deputy), but this task is assigned to the state secretary for European affairs. The pVEU is composed of representatives from all line ministries who are responsible for the European agenda, usually at the level of deputy ministers. Similarly to the vVEU, there are a number of associate members and permanent guests to the pVEU, including the representatives of the EU offices at both chambers of the Czech parliament. The secretariat of both the vVEU and pVEU is based at the office of the government and headed by the state secretary, who is, besides the chair of the pVEU, also the secretary of the vVEU. Thus, the coherence between the pVEU and vVEU is maintained through the person of the state secretary and his or her office.

At the lowest level, all ministries are obliged to create their RKS, which coordinates the European agenda within their respective field of responsibility and reports to the pVEU. The Statute of the VEU does not define the membership in the RKSs as a list (unlike the membership of the vVEU and pVEU respectively); rather it posits that representatives of all line ministries and governmental offices that have connection to the RKS's agenda should be members (Government of the Czech Republic, 2014b: Art. 10). In reality, this means that representatives of almost all line ministries are usually invited because the European agenda of an individual line ministry, as a rule, affects the business of most other sectors over the longer term. In addition, officials from various departments and sections within the ministry and representatives of subordinate organizations participate in the RKS's work, as well as officials from the permanent representation in Brussels (Interview #46; Interview #47). As a result, the architecture of the system ensures a high level of expertise at the working level, political authority at the higher levels, and communication across the whole government at all levels at the same time.

In practice, the pVEU, which meets every Tuesday, is the most important level for Czech EU policy-making. The vVEU meets only irregularly, depending on need, to solve disputes that could not be settled at the pVEU level, to adopt the mandates for European Council meetings, and to decide on dossiers that have been singled out by the prime minister and the government as highly politically sensitive and beyond the authority of the pVEU. The rest of the agenda is usually decided at the level of the pVEU, including the mandates for Council and COREPER I and II meetings. The RKSs prepare the work of the pVEU within their relevant area and are the ultimate decision-making level for individual instructions for Council working group meetings (cf. Souček, 2011).

The whole system relies on an electronic database labelled the Database of European policies (DAP). The DAP was established prior to the Czech Council presidency and evolved into both the means and space for Czech EU decision-making. The DAP contains all possible documents related to an individual EU dossier, including the original Commission/EEAS document, Czech evaluation, framework position, instructions and mandates, minutes from all types of related Council meetings, positions of other EU actors (where known), and relation to other EU and Czech documents. The agenda and background materials for the pVEU and RKSs' meetings are also circulated through the DAP and, if necessary, the actual decision-making can take place through the DAP too, usually by a silent procedure where the document is considered approved when no actor objects by a given deadline (which could be from several days to a few hours depending on the urgency). In fact, most of the RKSs of Czech line ministries work solely using the DAP and do not meet in person more than three to six times a year. The exceptions are the ministries of industry and trade, the environment, and agriculture where the RKSs meet every week in person (Interview #46; Interview #48).

"Framework positions" are the most important documents for the definition of the Czech national position in any EU negotiation (cf. Government of the Czech Republic, 2015b: 10). All European documents are received by the designated department at the office of the government, which uploads the document into the DAP and suggests a ministry that should be in charge of the agenda (the "administrator") and possible co-administrators (Government of the Czech Republic, 2014a). The administrator has the obligation to draft the framework position on the dossier, which is first discussed and adopted by the respective RKS and then approved by the pVEU (in some sensitive cases even the vVEU). The framework position serves as the basic document for the definition of Czech interests related to the dossier and the preferred results of the EU-level negotiations. It is supposed to be as detailed as possible in order to predict twists and shifts at the EU level, because it also serves as the basic framework for all related negotiation instructions and mandates (although it can be changed by the same procedure if the negotiations take an unexpected turn). In addition, the framework position is discussed by both chambers of the parliament according to their respective rules of procedure, i.e. mostly by the EU Affairs Committees and, where appropriate or necessary, by the plenary.

While the parliament is involved through the framework positions and informed by the parliament's officials participating as observers in the pVEU work, the non-state actors are at the same time less involved officially and fully involved in practice. Neither the status of the VEU, nor the rules of procedure lay down an obligation for the state representatives to reflect the opinions and interests of non-state actors. The status only prescribes that each RKS's status must define the 'mode and scope' of cooperation between the RKS and social partners, regions and municipalities, NGOs, and other relevant actors with a 'relationship to the discussed issues' (Government of the Czech Republic, 2014b: Art. 10). In reality, the RKS administrators and individual desk officers know the relevant non-state actors and they consult with them. Position papers by the non-state actors can then be included in the DAP as additional materials for the RKS and pVEU deliberation (Interview #47). This contrasts with the role of the parliament, particularly the Chamber of Deputies, which is stronger on paper, but quite inactive in practice (cf. Král and Bartovic, 2010).

Coordination of external policies

In principle, the coordination in EU external policies is not different from the standard procedure described in the previous paragraphs. The Statute of the VEU does not recognize any variation in procedure depending on the policy area. The key decisions are taken by the pVEU, sometimes by the vVEU, and the everyday agenda is managed by the RKSs of the respective line ministries.

Two ministries are most closely involved with the EU external relations agenda in the Czech Republic: the Ministry of Foreign Affairs of the Czech Republic (MFA) and the Ministry of Industry and Trade of the Czech Republic (MIT). While the former is responsible for the CFSP/CSDP agenda, enlargement, and neighbourhood policy, the latter is in charge of foreign trade. Other ministries, such as interior, defence, and justice, can be involved in some aspects of foreign relations, particularly in relation to migration and CSDP operations. Other sectorial policies also have their international aspects, such as climate negotiations on which the MIT coordinates with the Ministry of the Environment. Most of the time, the administrators of the bulk of the external agenda are the MFA and MIT.

The internal administration of the European agenda at the two ministries widely differs, which is at least partly related to the character of the issues that they process. The MIT looms large in the Czech European agenda because it is responsible for managing (at least partly) the Czech participation in three different formations of the Council – the Foreign Affairs Council (responsible for foreign trade), the Competitiveness Council (industry and the internal market), and the Transport, Telecommunications, and Energy Council (telecommunications and energy) (Ministry of Industry and Trade of the Czech Republic, 2015). The ministry's RKS is headed by the deputy minister for EU and foreign trade and administered by the Department for European Affairs and the Internal Market. As a consequence of the broad agenda, however, there are five sectorial working groups that report to the ministry's RKS and focus on particular aspects of the European agenda: energy, foreign trade, technical harmonization, competitiveness, and electronic communication and postal services. Each of these working groups acts as a small RKS with participation of relevant actors from other line ministries, the office of the government, the Brussels permanent representation, and subordinated institutions. They are also responsible for consulting their agenda with non-state actors that are active in their policy area.

At the MIT, most of the agenda consists of legislative proposals. There is therefore quite enough time to discuss and formulate the Czech positions. As already mentioned, the RKS at the MIT is one of only a few that actually meets in person every week, which is made easier by the fact that the decisions are not needed in a matter of hours. This does not mean, however, that the ministry needs a long time to adopt a position. As a standard time frame, the draft framework position on a given dossier is supposed to be uploaded into the DAP by Thursday, the ministry RKS discusses it on Monday, and on Tuesday it is already on the agenda of the pVEU (Interview #46). In case of urgency, this process can naturally be hastened by using the silent procedure in the DAP.

The Foreign Ministry is different in many respects, although it obviously should adhere to the procedure codified by the Status of the VEU in principle. Since the 'European Union provides an underlying framework for Czech foreign policy to be put into effect' (Government of the Czech Republic, 2015a), most of the Czech Foreign Ministry is in one way or another involved in European affairs. The ministry has a European Section, which beside geographical departments also hosts two departments specialized in the EU agenda, the EU General Affairs Department and the EU Policies and Structural Funds Department. The former is responsible for running the ministry's RKS, which relies on the DAP online environment and rarely meets in person.

Much of the ministry's agenda, however, particularly the non-legislative agenda in CFSP, does not have overlaps with other line ministries' business. Often, in addition, sensitive or even classified information is involved in these dossiers, such as within the scope of CSDP or human rights-related policies. Given the fact that the DAP is, even if not public, not certified to store classified information, the ministry does not use the database in these cases, nor does it involve the RKS. The cross-sectorial dialogue is substituted by an intra-ministry discussion among the horizontal and geographical departments as well as with the permanent representation in Brussels. If necessary, other line ministries are engaged on an ad hoc basis via individual consultations. Only politically very sensitive issues that require legitimation by the whole government are submitted to the VEU for approval.

As a result, there are multiple sections at the Foreign Ministry that are responsible for managing EU affairs in reality. Most notably, the Security and Multilateral Affairs Section is responsible for Czech policy within the CFSP (the CFSP Department) and CSDP (the Security Policy Department). The director of the CFSP Department is, at the same time, the Czech European correspondent, who serves as a contact point for CFSP-related communication between EU capitals, and the junior deputy minister in this section is the political director of the ministry. Moreover, the ministry hosts the Agent of the Czech Republic before the Court of the European Union appointed by the government following the foreign minister's proposal. The agent is aided by a separate committee with the participation of all ministries and the office of the government (Government of the Czech Republic, 2010).

In addition, the Foreign Ministry manages the permanent representation in Brussels, which is the key source of information for Czech EU policy-making and hub for interest promotion in the EU.[7] All permanent representation officials are Foreign Ministry employees, but some of them, particularly in sections dealing with sectorial policies, such as agriculture or foreign trade, are seconded from the line ministries – in these cases the Ministry of Agriculture and the MIT. The senior officials, usually with long diplomatic experience, come as a rule from the Foreign Ministry. The current permanent representative, for example, served as the political director of the ministry and as the permanent representative to NATO as well as ambassador to Chile and Spain in the past. In total, there are almost 100 officials working at the permanent representation, including assistants and secretaries. As a result, only one person is usually responsible for any given agenda. Sometimes one official must even cover the work of several working groups and this type of combination is particularly common in external relations, not necessarily connecting agendas with much relation to one another, such as transatlantic relations (COTRA) and Africa (COAFR) or Asia (COASI) and Latin America (COLAC) (Ministry of Foreign Affairs of the Czech Republic, 2015c). There is only one person responsible for the relations with the whole European Parliament and none covering the other institutions as such. All officials are expected to develop their own networks with relevant contacts at the EU institutions, but given their workload within the Council business it is difficult to imagine that they would be able to do so much beyond their immediate partners present at the working groups.

Understaffing is a general problem of Czech European policy, notably in foreign and security policy. Although there are specialized departments at the Foreign Ministry, they are not particularly large in terms of staff and they are responsible for a number of other issues beyond EU affairs. Taking the CFSP Department with 13 officials (as of August 2015) as an example: The department is responsible for coordinating the Czech positions in all CFSP matters and preparing instructions for the Political and Security Committee as well as the subordinate working groups. In addition, they manage the Czech link to COREU (an encrypted communication network for CFSP issues) and host the European correspondent. They also manage the Czech work in counter-terrorism within the CFSP, i.e. cooperate with the Czech intelligence services, organize reporting on international terrorism, and manage Czech participation in the Council working groups that deal with the external aspects of counter-terrorism. On top of that, the department is responsible for drafting positions on requests for armament export permits and checking their compliance with EU formal and informal regulations (Ministry of Foreign Affairs of the Czech Republic, 2015b). As a result, in the words of a senior ministry official, the CFSP positions and instructions are formally adopted in Prague, but the agenda is set and most of the business is managed in Brussels where 'a lot more people do it' (Interview #10).

Representation of Czech interests in external relations

People in Brussels and travelling to Brussels are instrumental in shaping the Czech interest promotion strategy. While the framework positions and instructions are adopted by the respective RKSs and the VEU in Prague, the particular negotiation tactics and the formal and informal activities that support the Czech position are not set centrally. In the end, it is the individuals representing the Czech Republic at the particular working groups and committees who, in cooperation with a handful of other officials in Brussels and in Prague, choose the most suitable way to promote Czech interests in a particular dossier. The strong role of the permanent representation in determining the Czech negotiation strategy is the result of their privileged access to information and their ability to see the broader picture (Interview #1). The permanent representation collects the bulk of information about other member states' positions and, naturally, about the positions of the Brussels institutions. Very limited information originates from bilateral embassies in other member states or the Heads of Missions (HoMs) meetings in third countries. Also given their continuous preoccupation with EU business they have a better overview of the context than the various desk officers in the capital who are responsible for their particular dossiers only.

As the case studies in this book suggest, in practice, the choice of a particular strategy rests with the individuals representing the Czech Republic in the particular working groups and committees (such as the COEST group and PSC or the TPC at various levels), the desk officer responsible for the agenda at the relevant line ministry (the MFA or MIT; in cases of capital-based working groups, this desk officer can also be the person participating in the actual meetings in Brussels), and one or two managing officers at the ministry who are regularly informed and must approve the selected activities (such as the deputy minister at the MIT and director general of the European section or the political director at the MFA). Among themselves, this group of people determine how the Czech interests, defined in the official process and set down by the framework position, are defended and promoted. Only occasionally do they reach out and engage other officials, most notably the minister, when the dossier reaches the Council level or when political endorsement in bilateral talks is required.

Naturally, there are many more people that determine the interest promotion strategies that go beyond a single dossier on the Council agenda. The cultivation of contact networks that serve as sources of early warning is the responsibility not only of the permanent representation officials, but of the whole ministry (or ministries) right from the minister down to the desk officers. The seeking of insider status is, in turn, first and foremost dependent on the domestic political debate and the resulting political choices (cf. Weiss, 2015a). But, in the end, even these more advanced strategies of interest promotion intersect in the selected group of officials who reap the results of the long-term efforts to strengthen the Czech negotiating position on a particular dossier.

Notes

1 It is worth mentioning that the act was adopted after intensive pressure from the European Commission that threatened to withhold European funds unless the act entered into force. The establishment of a civil service protected by a specific law had been a condition of the Czech EU accession. The respective act was indeed adopted by the Czech parliament in 2002, but it never entered into force and was substituted by a new law in 2014.
2 The only exception was the participation of Czech representatives in the Convention on the Future of Europe, which raised the public awareness of the ongoing debates

in the EU. Some conceptual documents were drafted, such as the Manifesto of Czech Eurorealism penned by a group of authors around the current MEP Jan Zahradil in April 2001.
3 The scepticism about the EU should be read in the context of Czech scepticism about institutions in general, including the national institutions, but even in this context a focus on the EU does not bring easy gains in popularity among voters.
4 A more detailed introduction of Czech interests in specific policy areas is part of the individual case studies.
5 All foreign policy concepts were adopted after Czech accession to NATO. However, the governmental programmes during the 1990s already identified NATO membership as 'an important tool for increasing Czech security' and planned to construct defence structures with the prospect of 'full integration with NATO and cooperation with the Western European Union' (Government of the Czech Republic, 1996).
6 Whereas the state secretary at the office of the government was appointed by a governmental decision at the time when the foreign minister's party abstained from governmental meetings due to inter-coalition disputes, the first deputy minister of foreign affairs received the title of state secretary by his minister's decision only.
7 In contrast to the practice at other ministries, there are no permanent representation officials participating in the work of the Foreign Ministry's RKS. The permanent representation is considered to be an internal part of the ministry, and as such, it participates in drafting the relevant documents before they are submitted to the formal approval procedure in the RKS (Interview #48).

3 Perceptions of Czech representatives in the Council of their work

A large part of the activities that member states' representatives undertake to promote national interests beyond the formal participation in Council meetings remains informal and does not leave behind any documents that could be studied. Any research on informal methods of interest promotion therefore has to rely on interviews with and surveys of direct participants.[1] This research combines both interviews with participants that feed into the exploration of individual case studies in the following chapters and a survey of Czech representatives in selected Council working groups and committees that have served in Brussels since 2003.[2]

The survey presented and analysed in this chapter addressed working groups contributing to the four policy areas studied in this research, namely foreign trade (the Article 133 Committee, later the Trade Policy Committee at the level of deputies), European Neighbourhood Policy (COEST, MaMa), human rights and democracy (COHOM), and Common Security and Defence Policy (CivCom, PMG), as well as the respective senior committees COREPER II and the Political and Security Committee with their preparatory groups Antici and Nicolaidis. The choice of the particular working groups and committees was based on the following logic: the four policy areas are represented at the working level by formations whose members reside in Brussels permanently as part of the permanent representation and contribute most extensively to the creation of a particular policy.[3] In addition, the more senior level was included (COREPER II, Antici, PSC, and Nicolaidis) to allow comparison between the working level that navigates within the framework of a single policy and the level at which several policy areas are covered simultaneously allowing for different negotiation styles and bringing more political clout to the table. Covering the period between 2003 and 2015, the survey also allows for comparison across time to capture whether the Czech administration has changed its working methods in Brussels.

In the questionnaire, which is shown in full in Table 3.1 translated into English, the respondents were asked to evaluate their own work in Brussels and to state how often they used the listed tools and working methods (question 5). Next, they were requested to identify the most important tools and activities that helped a state of the Czech Republic's size to promote and block proposals out of the list already used in the previous question

Table 3.1 Questionnaire

Question 1. In which of these working groups/committees did you serve? Please choose the one to which you contributed the most.

[ ] COREPER II [ ] Antici [ ] COPS/PSC [ ] Nicolaidis [ ] COHOM
[ ] COEST [ ] MaMa [ ] Article 133 Committee/TPC [ ] CivCom [ ] PMG

Question 2. When did you start contributing to the creation of European policies directly in Brussels within the framework of the working group/committee chosen in the previous question? ....

Question 3. When did you finish contributing to the creation of European policies directly in Brussels within the framework of the working group/committee from question 1? ....

Question 4. How many years had you served in diplomacy or a related sector of public administration before working in Brussels at the working group/committee chosen in the first question? ....

In the following questions, we will ask about your work in the working group/committee that you referred to in the previous questions 1–4.

Question 5.1. Which of the following options best describes how often you used the following tools or participated in the following activities in your work?

	For (almost) every discussed issue	Several times a month	Several times a year	Less often	Never
Informal consultations or meetings with other member states' representatives	( )	( )	( )	( )	( )
Efforts to win support of one of the big member states	( )	( )	( )	( )	( )
Consultations with the Commission	( )	( )	( )	( )	( )
Consultations with the EEAS/presidency	( )	( )	( )	( )	( )
Contact with Czechs (or other friendly nationalities) in EU institutions	( )	( )	( )	( )	( )
Authoring or co-authoring non-papers	( )	( )	( )	( )	( )

Participation in like-minded groups	( )	( )	( )	( )	( )
Organization of like-minded groups	( )	( )	( )	( )	( )
Contact with non-state actors (businesses, NGOs)	( )	( )	( )	( )	( )
Organization of expert events (e.g. seminars)	( )	( )	( )	( )	( )
Organization of social events (e.g. dinners)	( )	( )	( )	( )	( )

Question 5.2. And how often did you use the following tools or participate in the following activities in your work?

	For (almost) every discussed issue	Several times a month	Several times a year	Less often	Never
Contact with MEPs	( )	( )	( )	( )	( )
Lobbying through a Commissioner/ High Representative and their cabinets	( )	( )	( )	( )	( )
Issue linkage and exchange of support with other states	( )	( )	( )	( )	( )
Threat of blocking the consensus and referring the issue to a higher level	( )	( )	( )	( )	( )
Blocking the consensus and referring the issue to a higher level	( )	( )	( )	( )	( )

Persuading partners with arguments	( )	( )	( )	( )	( )
Formulating/ describing the Czech position as a proposal that is in the European interest	( )	( )	( )	( )	( )
Involving the capital in negotiations (e.g. the political director, deputy minister, minister etc.)	( )	( )	( )	( )	( )
Searching for additional information about the negotiated issues (increasing expertise)	( )	( )	( )	( )	( )
Specialization within the policy area on selected issues	( )	( )	( )	( )	( )
Raising public awareness about own preferences and priority areas (e.g. through the media)	( )	( )	( )	( )	( )

Question 5.3. Did you use any other important tool in your work that was not mentioned above?

	For (almost) every discussed issue	Several times a month	Several times a year	Less often	Never
Other (please add):	( )	( )	( )	( )	( )
Other (please add):	( )	( )	( )	( )	( )

Question 6. Select up to five tools/activities that you consider most important for a successful effort by a member state of the Czech Republic's size to PROMOTE its own proposal in the policy area in which you participated.

[ ] Informal consultations or meetings with other member states' representatives
[ ] Efforts to win support of one of the big member states
[ ] Consultations with the Commission
[ ] Consultations with the EEAS/presidency
[ ] Contact with Czechs (or other friendly nationalities) in EU institutions
[ ] Authoring or co-authoring non-papers
[ ] Participation in like-minded groups
[ ] Organization of like-minded groups
[ ] Contact with non-state actors (businesses, NGOs)
[ ] Organization of business events (e.g. seminars)
[ ] Organization of social events (e.g. dinners)
[ ] Contact with MEPs
[ ] Lobbying through a Commissioner/High Representative and their cabinets
[ ] Issue linkage and exchange of support with other states
[ ] Threat of blocking the consensus and referring the issue to a higher level
[ ] Blocking the consensus and referring the issue to a higher level
[ ] Persuading partners with arguments
[ ] Formulating/describing the Czech position as a proposal that is in the European interest
[ ] Involving the capital in negotiations (e.g. the political director, deputy minister, minister etc.)
[ ] Searching for additional information about the negotiated issues (increasing expertise)
[ ] Specialization within the policy area on selected issues
[ ] Raising public awareness about own preferences and priority areas (e.g. through the media)

Question 7. Select up to five tools/activities that you consider most important for a successful effort of a member state of the Czech Republic's size to BLOCK a proposal in the policy area in which you participated.

[ ] Informal consultations or meetings with other member states' representatives
[ ] Efforts to win support of one of the big member states
[ ] Consultations with the Commission
[ ] Consultations with the EEAS/presidency
[ ] Contact with Czechs (or other friendly nationalities) in EU institutions
[ ] Authoring or co-authoring non-papers
[ ] Participation in like-minded groups
[ ] Organization of like-minded groups
[ ] Contact with non-state actors (businesses, NGOs)
[ ] Organization of business events (e.g. seminars)
[ ] Organization of social events (e.g. dinners)
[ ] Contact with MEPs
[ ] Lobbying through a Commissioner/High Representative and their cabinets
[ ] Issue linkage and exchange of support with other states
[ ] Threat of blocking the consensus and referring the issue to a higher level
[ ] Blocking the consensus and referring the issue to a higher level
[ ] Persuading partners with arguments
[ ] Formulating/describing the Czech position as a proposal that is in the European interest

[ ] Involving the capital in negotiations (e.g. the political director, deputy minister, minister etc.)
[ ] Searching for additional information about the negotiated issues (increasing expertise)
[ ] Specialization within the policy area on selected issues
[ ] Raising public awareness about own preferences and priority areas (e.g. through the media)

Question 8. Order the following factors according to their importance for the promotion of Czech interests in the policy area in which you participated. Place the most important factor at the top and the least important factor at the bottom.

[ ] Czech expertise in the individual dossier
[ ] Personal qualities of the negotiator
[ ] State size (population, economy)
[ ] Good coordination between the permanent representation and the central offices in Prague
[ ] Positive image of the Czech Republic
[ ] Active participation of the Czech Republic in the issue area (e.g. bilateral connections, private and public investments, Czech participation in related EU activities etc.)
[ ] Fellow countrymen in key positions in European institutions (Commission, Parliament, EEAS)
[ ] Timely access to information on proposals in preparation
[ ] Other (add below in question 8.1): ...

Question 8.1. Please list other factors from the previous question 8 here. ....

Question 9. Order the following factors according to how they prevent the Czech Republic from being more successful in the promotion of its own interests. Place the biggest obstacle at the top and the smallest obstacle at the bottom.

[ ] Insufficient Czech expertise in the individual dossier
[ ] Insufficient personal qualities of the negotiator
[ ] State size (population, economy)
[ ] Bad coordination between the permanent representation and the central offices in Prague
[ ] Negative image of the Czech Republic
[ ] Insufficient participation of the Czech Republic in the issue area (e.g. bilateral connections, private and public investments, Czech participation in related EU activities etc.)
[ ] Lack of fellow countrymen in key positions in European institutions (Commission, Parliament, EEAS)
[ ] Late access to information on proposals in preparation
[ ] Other (add below in question 9.1): ...

Question 9.1. Please list other factors from the previous question 9 here. ....

Question 10. Do you currently work on European affairs within the Czech public administration?

[ ] Yes [ ] No

(questions 6 and 7). The last two substantive questions focused on factors that the respondents considered important for the promotion of Czech interests in their respective policy area (question 8) and factors that hindered Czech performance (question 9). All of the questions 5–9 worked with a pre-defined list of tools and factors, but in questions 5, 8, and 9 the respondents could add their own tool or factor that they considered important but could not find on the list. In questions 4 and 10, the respondents were asked about their career before and after their posting in Brussels. More specifically, they were asked to state how many years they had served in diplomacy or a related branch of public administration before they left for Brussels, and whether they worked on European affairs for the Czech public service at the time of the questionnaire.

While a survey is a useful tool to gather data that would otherwise be unavailable, it brings about a number of limitations that need to be taken into consideration. First and foremost, there is the issue of validity. It is crucial that the respondents approach the questionnaire with different personal experience and understanding interpreting the individual questions and answers as coherently as possible. That is why the frequency modes in question 5 were set down in absolute terms and subjective categories such as "often" and "rarely", which may have a different meaning in various policy areas, were avoided. In any case, it should be stated clearly that the data presented below do not represent "objective" facts, but the perceptions of officials representing the Czech Republic in the Council of their work and of the factors that are significant in EU policy-making. There is no way to double-check or triangulate any of the responses and it is necessary to rely on the respondents, i.e. that when agreeing to fill in the form, they did so in the most precise way according to their best knowledge and assessment.

The reliance on respondents' assessments is even more important given the very limited population on which the survey could be conducted. Fewer than 50 persons have served in Brussels on behalf of the Czech Republic in the selected working groups and committees since 2003. Consequently, every single response (and it needs to be noted that not everybody did respond, see below) is able to shift the ratios between results, especially when the respondents are divided into smaller groups according to policy area, seniority, or time in order to allow for comparison. As a result, the conclusions of the survey should not be overestimated. A much more robust survey would be required to provide more conclusive results, ideally with a cross-country element, which was beyond the capacity of the present research. Nevertheless, despite all the limitations the results offer interesting insight into the practice of a single member state, and as such, they are useful for refining the working hypotheses and outlining directions for further research projects.

Collection period, response rate, and structure of respondents

The survey was prepared using a professional online survey tool. The first request for answers was sent out in July 2015 and the collection ended in

September 2015 with two reminders being sent out in between. The list of respondents was identified in cooperation with the Foreign Ministry and the Czech permanent representation in Brussels. The email addresses of those individuals that had left the Foreign Ministry in the meantime were collected from their former colleagues where possible. In total, 44 individuals were identified that have served on the respective working groups and committees on behalf of the Czech Republic since 2003 (with several of them working in two different positions during their time in Brussels). Contact details of two of them were impossible to obtain, either through the ministry or from their former colleagues, and as a result, 42 individual questionnaires were sent out. By the end of the collection period, 30 completed questionnaires were gathered, which equals a response rate of 71.42 per cent.

Unsurprisingly, it was easier to contact those officials who were still serving in Brussels or had left Brussels only recently and more difficult to obtain answers from those who had worked at the Czech permanent representation in Brussels further in the past. As a result, only three of the respondents concluded their stay in Brussels in 2004, none of them in the period 2005–2008, and the rest between 2009 and 2014, or were still serving in Brussels in 2015.[4] The distribution is shown in Figure 3.1. While ten respondents represented the Czech Republic at the senior Council level, comprising COREPER II, PSC, Antici, and Nicolaidis, the remaining 20 respondents served at the working level (TPC, COEST, MaMa, COHOM, CivCom, and PMG) (see Figure 3.2).

On average, the respondents have spent 3.37 years in their respective Council working group or committee with a median value equal to 3.5 years.

Experience of Czech diplomats posted in Brussels

Similar to other diplomatic representations abroad, the permanent representation in Brussels offers positions for junior and senior diplomats alike. The Council working groups and committees vary in terms of seniority and while the ambassadors to the COREPER II or the PSC are usually experienced diplomats, the member states may be represented by less experienced diplomats in the more junior working groups.[5] The diplomats' level of seniority may be determined by the tradition in the Council to some extent, but it mainly can be understood as a function of the significance the member state's foreign policy attaches to its performance in the working group. Two alternative expectations can be formulated in this respect, one based on policy preference and the other on the character of the work in the working group. First, the more important the policy area is for the member state, the more experienced diplomats will be deployed to represent national policy in the Council. Alternatively, the more demanding it will be to secure national interests in the particular working group, the more experienced diplomats will be sent to represent the member state.

Securing national interests in foreign trade and ENP should be considered more difficult than in democracy and human rights and CSDP given the qualified majority decision-making on many issues and the bigger involvement of

42 *Perceptions of Czech representatives*

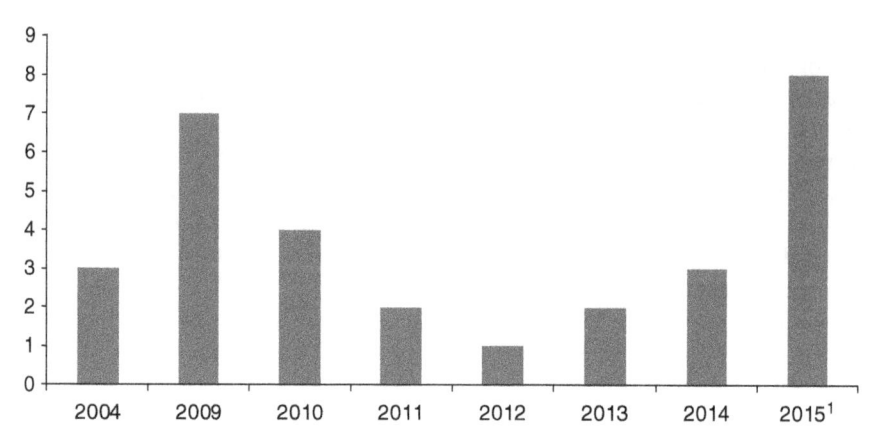

Figure 3.1 Number of respondents according to the year they finished their tenure in Brussels

Note: [1] These respondents either concluded their stay or were still serving in Brussels in 2015.

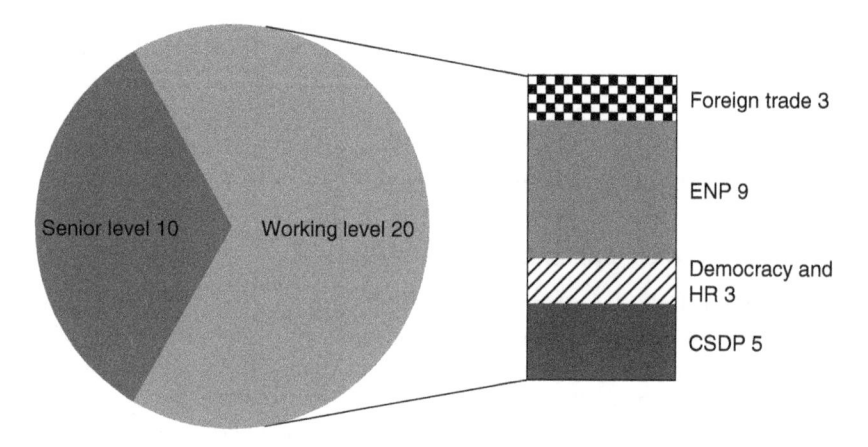

Figure 3.2 Number of respondents according to the level of the working group and policy area

EU institutions. On the other hand, the Czech Republic has an explicit interest in ENP and democracy and human rights promotion, unlike in foreign trade and CSDP where it has traditionally been present, but has not identified either of these areas as a priority. The varying experience of Czech diplomats deployed to Brussels to individual working groups and committees can thus offer guidance on what plays a role when the Czech Foreign Ministry evaluates a suitable candidate. The data shown in the tables offer an overview of how many years the respondents served in diplomacy or a related area of public administration before their deployment to the Czech permanent representation to the EU.

Table 3.2 Previous experience in diplomacy or related area of public administration I (in years)

	Average	Median	Maximum	Minimum
All	7.7	8	22	0
Senior level	9.5	9.5	22	2
Working level	6.8	6	20	0

Table 3.3 Previous experience in diplomacy or related area of public administration II (in years)

	Average	Median	Maximum	Minimum
Foreign trade	10	6	20	4
ENP	7.1	7	14	0
Democracy and HR	5	3	10	2
CSDP	5.4	4	9	3

The data reveal (see Table 3.2) that indeed there is a significant difference in the average and median number of years served between the senior level and the working level representatives. At the same time, however, there is no significant difference between the maximum and minimum number of years. In other words, while generally more experienced people represent the Czech Republic at the senior level than at the working level, there are examples of very experienced individuals posted to the working level and rather inexperienced individuals being sent to serve at the senior level.

When divided according to the policy area at the working level (see Table 3.3), the data suggest that the decision-making style is important for the Czech Republic when sending out representatives to Brussels, rather than the foreign policy priority. Both the average and median values for foreign trade and ENP are significantly higher than for democracy and human rights and CSDP. Indeed, on democracy and human rights promotion, which is one of the most explicit priorities for Czech foreign policy, the Czech Republic has been represented by the least experienced diplomats of all.

Methods and tools for Czech interest promotion

The first working hypothesis of this research expects that the number of different methods that the country's negotiators use to promote national interests increases over time. This is a result of the learning that is connected with EU membership; only when familiarized with the environment in the EU can the country use the full range of methods to influence the negotiations. In order to test this simple hypothesis, the methods that the respondents marked

44 *Perceptions of Czech representatives*

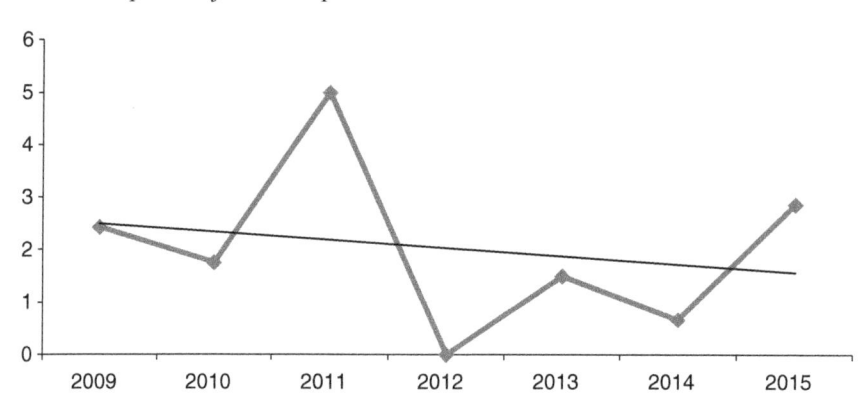

Figure 3.3 Average number of methods "never" used according to year. Data for the year 2004 are not included

as "never" being used were counted and compared across time, using the end of the Brussels tenure as the key.

The data reveal (see Figure 3.3) that, indeed, Czech representatives tend to use on average ever more methods. The data fluctuate a lot, however. In addition, if the year 2004 is added where the average number of unused methods for interest promotion was 1, the trend line reverses and shows a slight increase.

In this research, the methods and tools for interest promotion are divided into three groups according to the level of sophistication. All methods were identified either in the literature on lobbying and interest promotion in the EU, in the literature on EU decision-making, or during preliminary interviews with stakeholders from various member states and EU institutions. The first group comprises methods that focus on an individual dossier that is negotiated in the Council. It is considered the least sophisticated, because it mirrors the standard negotiation style in common international organizations and reflects the specific conditions in the EU very little. The second group consists of methods that the member states' representatives may use to collect information about the agenda in order to prepare in advance, refine their negotiation position, draw fall-back scenarios, and prepare arguments. The third group, which is considered the most sophisticated, includes methods that the member states may use to gain "insider status", i.e. to become a recognized stakeholder in a particular issue and to be invited into the inner circles of those that prepare and pre-discuss draft proposals. Table 3.4 shows the distribution of the methods analysed in the survey into the three groups.

The working research hypotheses 2 and 3 expected that the use of more sophisticated methods would increase both over time and across policy areas depending directly on the level of involvement of EU institutions and indirectly on the decreasing power of a single state to block policy initiatives. These expectations result from the following logic. First, group 2 and group 3

Table 3.4 Distribution of methods of interest promotion into three groups

Group 1 methods	Group 2 methods	Group 3 methods
Informal consultations or meetings with other member states' representatives	Consultations with the Commission	Organization of like-minded groups
Efforts to win support of one of the big member states	Consultations with the EEAS/presidency	Contact with non-state actors (businesses, NGOs)
Authoring or co-authoring non-papers	Contact with Czechs (or other friendly nationalities) in EU institutions	Organization of expert events (e.g. seminars)
Participation in like-minded groups	Organization of social events (e.g. dinners)	Searching for additional information about the negotiated issues (increasing expertise)
Contact with MEPs		Specialization within the policy area on selected issues
Lobbying through a Commissioner/High Representative and their cabinets		Raising public awareness about own preferences and priority areas (e.g. through the media)
Issue linkage and exchange of support with other states		
Threat of blocking the consensus and referring the issue to a higher level		
Blocking the consensus and referring the issue to a higher level		
Persuading partners with arguments		
Formulating/describing the Czech position as a proposal that is in the European interest		
Involving the capital in negotiations (e.g. the political director, deputy minister, minister etc.)		

methods are more effective in securing national interests in the longer term.[6] As a result, it can be assumed that the more member states understand how the EU works internally, i.e. the longer they are members, the more they use methods and tools that belong to groups 2 and 3. Second, the member states need to be more active and aim at using the broadest spectrum of methods

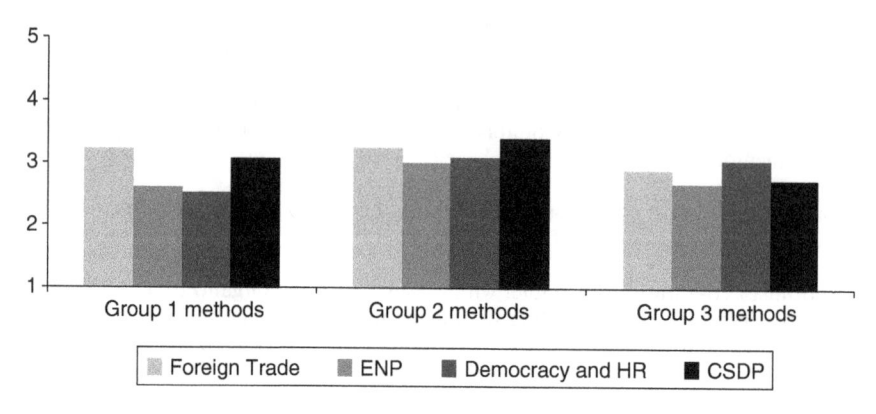

Figure 3.4 Use of interest promotion methods in individual policy areas. The values on the y-axis correspond to the following options in the questionnaire: 5 = for (almost) every discussed issue; 4 = several times a month; 3 = several times a year; 2 = less often; 1 = never

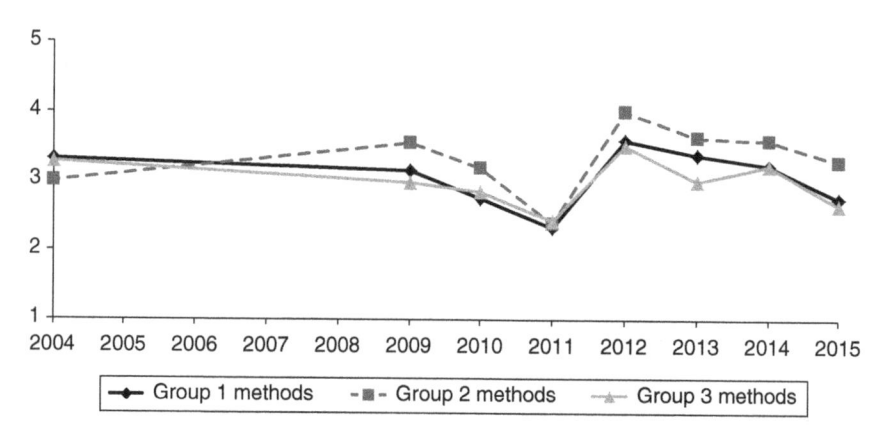

Figure 3.5 Use of interest promotion methods over time. The values on the y-axis correspond to the following options in the questionnaire: 5 = for (almost) every discussed issue; 4 = several times a month; 3 = several times a year; 2 = less often; 1 = never

and tools where they cannot rely on the formal procedures to secure their interests, most notably in policy areas in which they can be outvoted in the Council. Similarly, where there is a strong role for the European Commission and the European Parliament, the power of the Council itself is limited and the member states cannot rely solely on Council negotiations and need to be active in the preparatory phases of the European policy cycle as well, especially by acquiring timely information and by an effort to become insiders.

There are some qualifications to these assumptions, though. First of all, the learning curve cannot continue indefinitely. At some point in time, the member state's representation would probably "understand" how the EU works and use all the types of methods according to the needs of the particular situation. Thus, while there would be growing use of the more sophisticated methods after the accession and during the first years of membership, the growth would level out at a particular time. Second, a country does not need to be an insider on all issues. As a matter of fact, the whole logic of interest promotion in the EU suggests that smaller member states would concentrate their capacities on those issues that concern their respective priorities and more or less ignore other dossiers. That means that there is limited room for a more intensive use of the group 3 methods in absolute terms. Smaller member states will not be able to become insiders on every dossier or several times every month; they will concentrate their forces on becoming insiders in cases of high salience.

The survey results do not support the research hypotheses in a conclusive manner. Indeed, there is variation in the frequency with which the Czech representatives employ different methods, but this cannot be ascribed to time or policy area. Figure 3.4 shows that the group 1 and group 2 methods are used in foreign trade and in CSDP the most: that is, the two policy areas that are most different from each other in terms of decision-making and involvement of other EU institutions. Group 3 methods are, in turn, most used in democracy and human rights policy together with foreign trade and least used in ENP.

Similarly, no obvious learning curve can be identified when evaluating the Czech performance over time. Figure 3.5 reveals that although there has been variation in the frequency with which the Czech representatives in the Council employed different methods over time, no clear increase can be traced in either of the groups. Moreover, when compared to the "rookie" situation of 2004, the data show stagnation or even a decrease in sophistication in the Czech performance. There is one exception, however, which concerns the group 2 methods. The data suggest that whereas the "early warning" methods were the least used in 2004, they became the most frequent tools of interest promotion for Czech Council representatives. This leads to the conclusion that Czech negotiators have learnt the value of timely information and have started using methods that aim at information gathering.

There are some additional conclusions that can be drawn from the data. First of all, the level of negotiation seems to matter when the activity of Czech representatives is concerned. Figure 3.6 clearly shows that Czech negotiators at more senior levels tend to use all types of methods much more often than their colleagues at the working level. The difference is largest in group 1 methods, which can be explained rather easily. While the agenda at the working level often includes dossiers that are unproblematic and just need to be discussed and agreed, the senior level deals mainly with agendas that could not be satisfactorily concluded at lower levels. Therefore, most dossiers at this level contain a certain dispute that needs to be removed by negotiation and the higher frequency of methods focused on particular dossiers is only logical. Correspondingly, the more common use of elaborate methods can be explained following the same logic: the more contested an issue becomes,

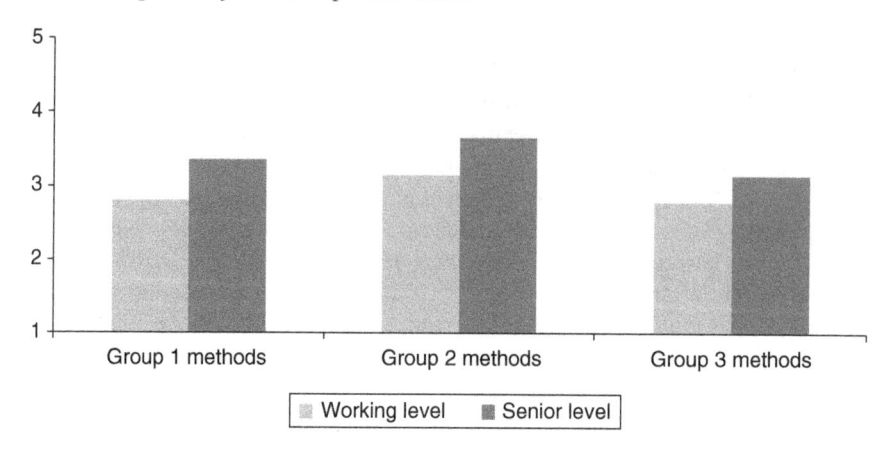

Figure 3.6 Use of interest promotion methods at different negotiation levels. The values on the y-axis correspond to the following options in the questionnaire: 5 = for (almost) every discussed issue; 4 = several times a month; 3 = several times a year; 2 = less often; 1 = never

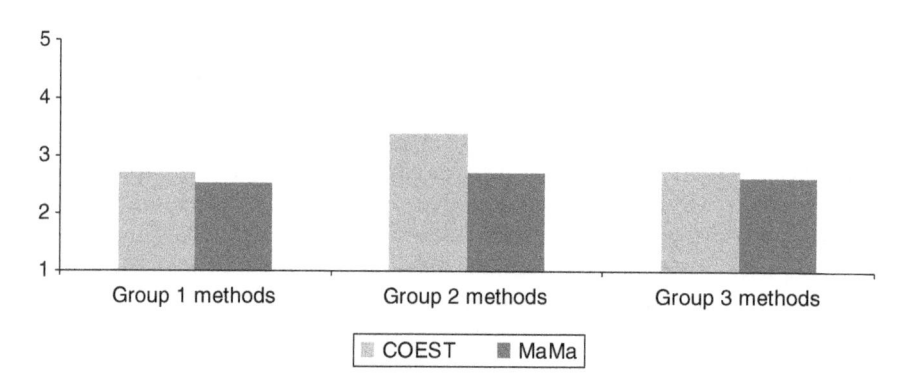

Figure 3.7 Use of interest promotion methods in European Neighbourhood Policy. The values on the y-axis correspond to the following options in the questionnaire: 5 = for (almost) every discussed issue; 4 = several times a month; 3 = several times a year; 2 = less often; 1 = never

the more useful it is to get timely information or even to be invited to smaller groups where the compromise is hammered out.

Second, policy salience contributes to higher use of the interest promotion methods. Figure 3.7 compares the use of interest promotion methods between the two directions of European Neighbourhood Policy as represented by the two geographic working groups, COEST and MaMa. While the Czech Republic has only limited interest in the MaMa's target area, North Africa and the Middle East, Eastern Europe, which is the focus of COEST work, belongs to Czech foreign policy priorities. Since the institutional setting remains more or less the same for both directions of the ENP, variation in methods would suggest that the policy interest directly influences the activity of the country's negotiators. The data show that there is, indeed, a significant difference between the levels of activity in the two working groups. The difference is largest in the group 2 methods, i.e. in methods that help acquire timely information about future negotiations, but it is visible in all three groups.

What respondents consider important and how this is reflected in their work

Besides being asked to evaluate how they have used individual tools in their work, the respondents should identify tools they consider important for a member state of the Czech Republic's size to promote and block proposals in the EU. As the figures in this section show, there are major differences between the individual tools' perceived value in promoting a member state's preferred position and in blocking undesirable results. Similarly, officials serving at the senior level value some tools differently than those active at the working level.

Taking into account all respondents first, Figure 3.8 shows that tools valued for their ability to help a member state promote its preferred policy option, particularly informal consultations with other member states and with the EEAS or presidency, are considered much less important for the ability to block. The same is true for non-papers and for contacts with compatriots in EU institutions. In contrast, support of a big member state and the involvement of the capital are considered much more important for their negative power than for their capacity to promote preferred policy. That also applies to lobbying through the Commissioners or their cabinets.

The data also reveal that, rather unsurprisingly, threatening to block and actual blocking of consensus in the Council are considered important for the member state's ability to obstruct decisions. At the same time, obstructions have very limited value in promoting the positive agenda. This seems to be in line with accounts of EU policy-making, suggesting that a positive and club-like approach is necessary to push one's own interests through the Council (cf. Juncos and Pomorska, 2008). Formulation of a national interest as a European interest seems, however, not to bring a country's representative very far either when promoting or blocking the agenda, according to the respondents (contrast with Panke, 2010b: 25ff.).

There are significant differences between distinct levels of negotiation in the Council when it comes to methods perceived as important to promote one's position (see Figure 3.9). First, the consultations with the Commission, the EEAS, and the presidency are considered more important at the working level, while coalition building and argumentation (including framing as a European interest) are valued more at the senior level. At the working level, a broader range of tools is considered valuable at least by some respondents. What also should be noted is that threatening to block a consensus is

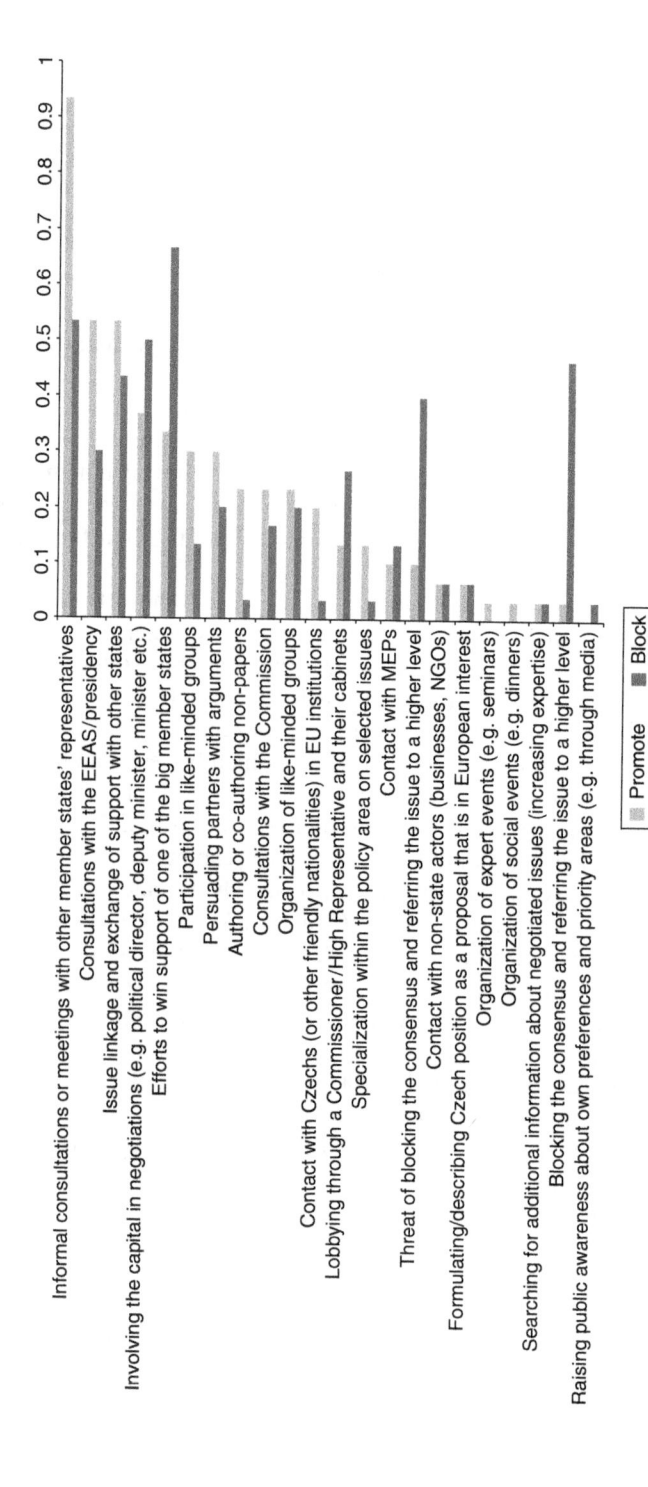

Figure 3.8 Perceived value of tools for promoting or blocking a proposal

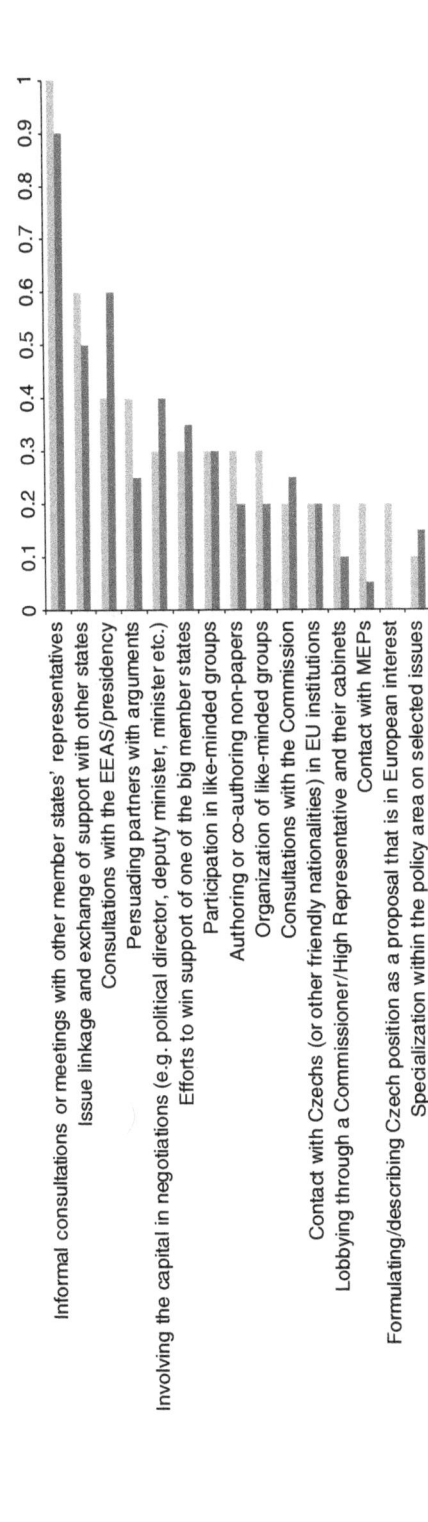

Figure 3.9 Perceived value of tools for promoting a proposal at different levels

considered a relatively important tool to push forward a positive agenda at the working level, but is not considered an option at all at the senior level. In contrast, senior level representatives recognize the importance of contacts with the MEPs much more than working level officials.

Similar differences can be recognized in the Czech representatives' assessment of the individual methods' value for blocking an undesired proposal (see Figure 3.10). While some tools are given a similar high value, in particular winning support of a big state, involving the capital, and consultations with other member states, assessment of other methods shows striking differences. While 40 per cent of senior level respondents considered participation in like-minded groups important for the state's ability to block an undesired proposal, none of the working level respondents thought so. On other issues, the difference between the senior and working level assessment was a full 25 percentage points: for example, issue linkage is valued more at the senior level, while lobbying through the Commissioners and their cabinets as well as blocking of consensus and referring the issue to a higher level was considered more important at the working level.

A lot of these variations can be ascribed to the different negotiation styles at the working and senior levels that are closely linked to the agenda. At the senior level, politically contested issues are discussed mostly and as a result, more coalition building and bargaining takes place. At the working level, in contrast, the state's representatives are usually confronted with the proposals for the first time and therefore tend to need more contacts with the agenda-setters, particularly the Commission and the EEAS/presidency.

The role of the big states is, on the other hand, regarded similarly at both negotiation levels. Big states' support is apparently considered crucial for the state's ability to block an undesired proposal. What is more interesting is the fact that the big states are not considered as important for the promotion of a positive agenda (a difference of about 35 percentage points). This suggests that size has a different value dependent on the negotiation situation and while it helps significantly to prevent creation of a European policy that is unwanted, it is of lesser advantage when it comes to promoting a preferred option (compare with the assessment of "size" as a factor in the next section).

Having analysed both the Czech negotiators' assessment of their work and the value of individual tools, it is now time to ask whether their activities reflect their convictions. Figure 3.11 shows correlation coefficients for both the positive (promoting) and negative (blocking) value of the tools. In general, it can be stated that where there is a stronger correlation, it is mostly positive. That means that Czech representatives largely focus on the tools that they consider important and do not use tools they see as useless. At the same time, however, none of the correlations is particularly strong. It is, therefore, not possible to claim that the Czech representatives are deliberately considering some methods of interest promotion as important according to them, while ignoring others completely.

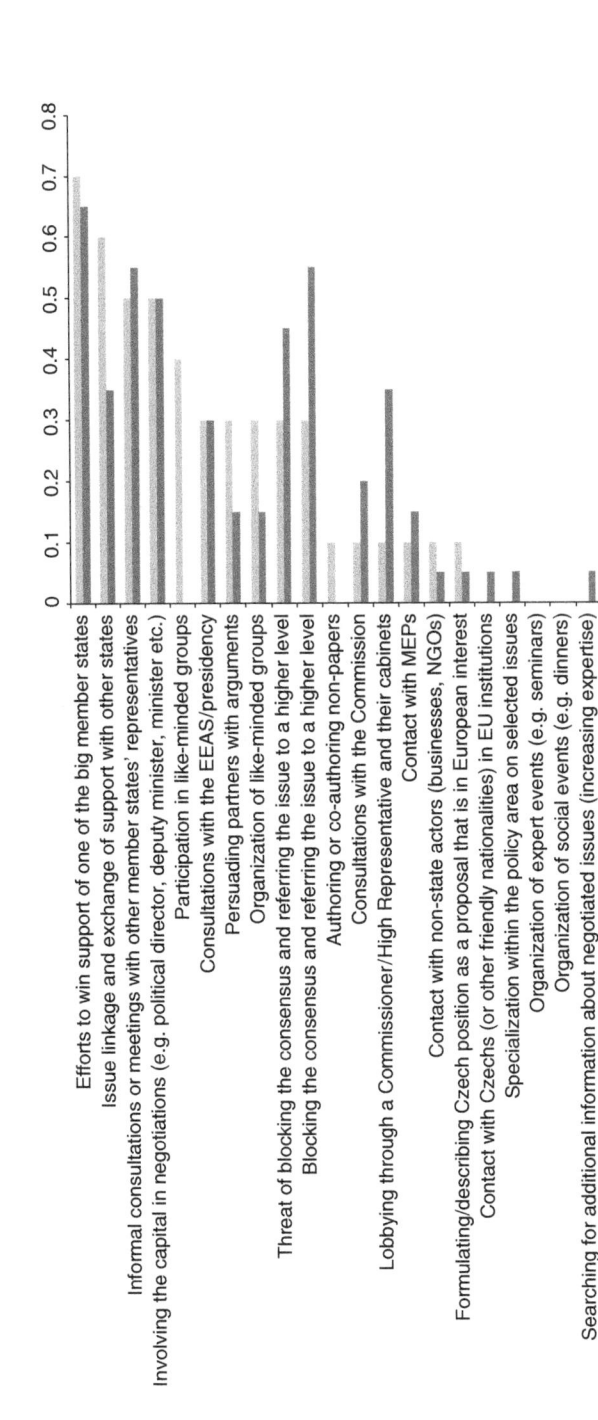

Figure 3.10 Perceived value of tools for blocking a proposal at different levels

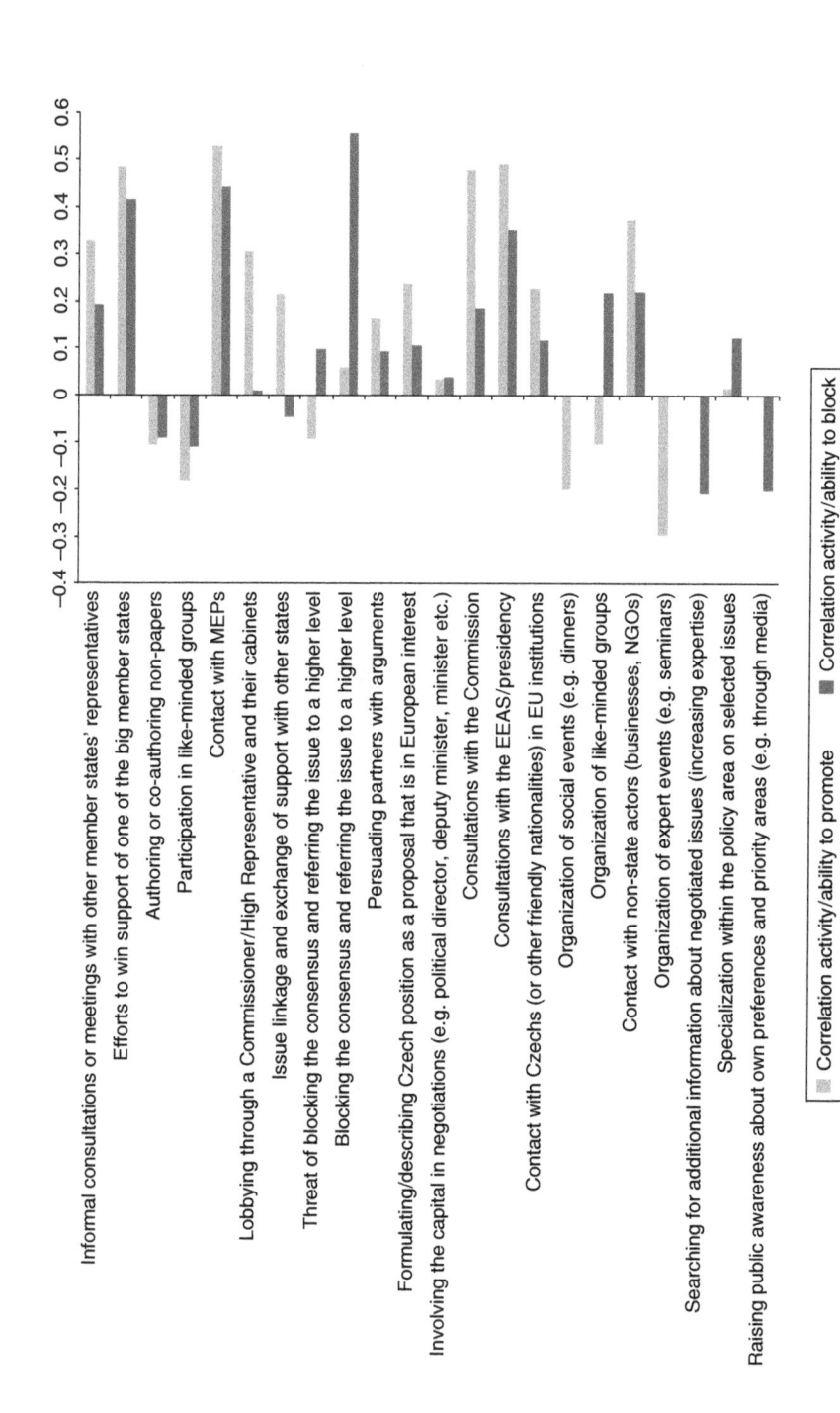

Figure 3.11 Correlation between the Czech representatives' activity and what they perceive as important for promoting and blocking agendas

Perceptions of Czech representatives 55

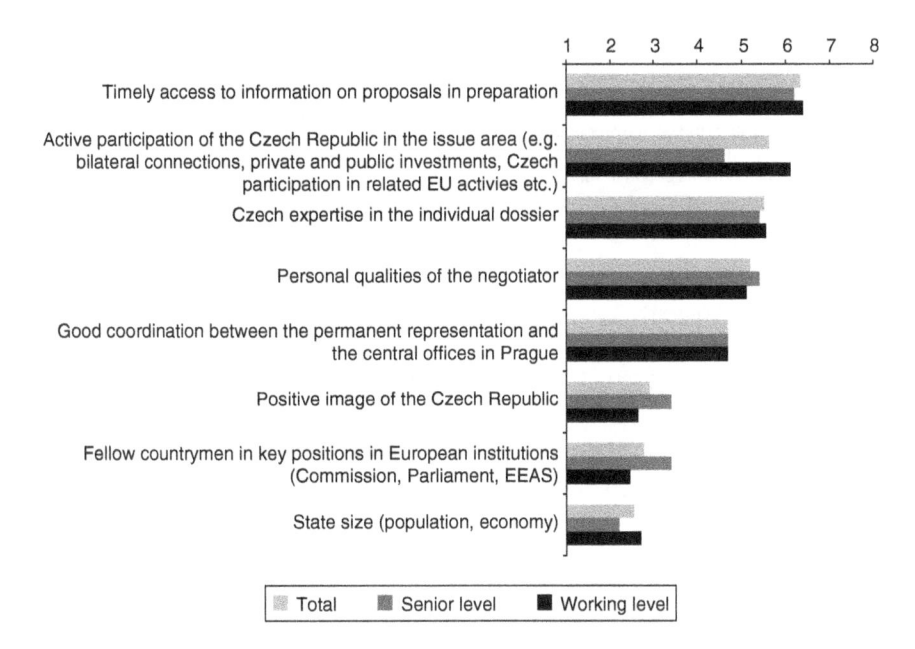

Figure 3.12 Factors' importance for promoting Czech influence (average)

Factors influencing Czech success in EU negotiations

The activities of a state's representatives in the Council are by no means the only factors that decide whether a country is successful in promoting its national interests. Therefore, the survey also addressed the issue of other factors, partly external to the respondent's work or independent from it, and asked for their assessment both in terms of importance and in terms of the Czech performance in these factors. As with the rest of the questionnaire, these factors were extracted from the literature on EU decision-making. The respondents could identify additional factors if they felt that an important issue was missing.

The results show that timely access to information is considered the most important factor, followed by active Czech participation in the issue area and expertise (see Figure 3.12).[7] This is in accordance with the lobbying literature that emphasizes access to information and engagement as the crucial factors for a lobbyist to make a change. The country's size is, on the other hand, considered the least important factor by the Czech negotiators, thus concurring with some in academia who play down the role of power in EU decision-making. When broken down according to policy area (see Figure 3.13), the juxtaposition of expertise and size becomes even more apparent. In general, there is no significant difference in the results between policy areas. The respondents active in the democracy and human rights area, however, put much greater emphasis on expertise than others and, at the same time, valued the state's size much less.

56 Perceptions of Czech representatives

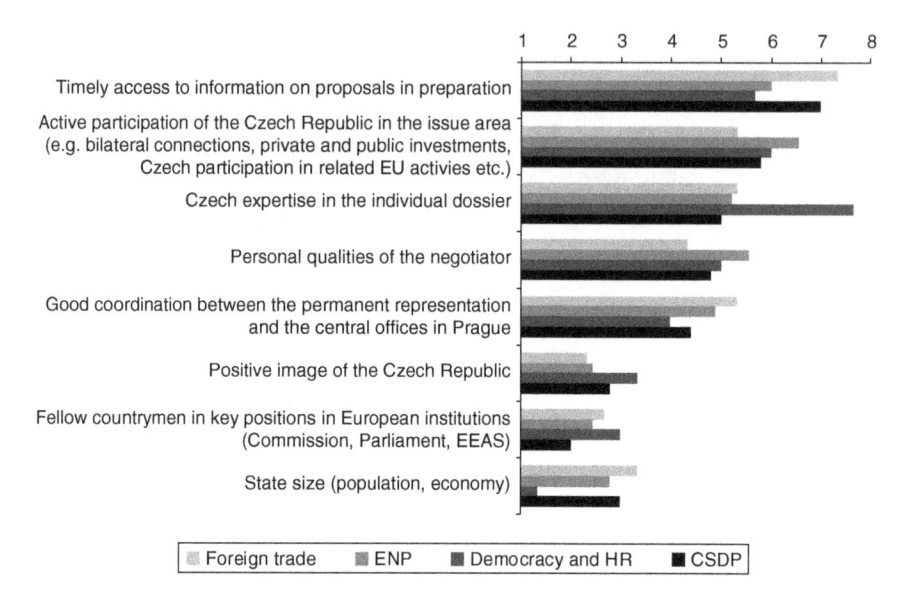

Figure 3.13 Factors' importance for promoting Czech influence according to policy area (average)

There are no significant differences between the responses of Czech negotiators at the working and senior levels, with a few exceptions. At the working level, both active participation and the country's size are considered more important. In contrast, fellow countrymen and the country's positive image are valued more at the senior level. These differences can be partly interpreted as a result of the distinct character of negotiation at various levels, particularly the emphasis on active participation at the working level and on the country's image at the senior level. In other cases, such interpretation would be more difficult; we could expect size to loom larger at the senior level where the bargaining takes place over politically contested issues. The differences should not be overestimated, however, because the respondents were asked about their evaluation of the factors in general, not for their personal activities. Overall, moreover, there is general agreement between the two levels about what is more important (e.g. access to information, expertise, and active participation) and less important (e.g. size, fellow countrymen, and positive image).

Interestingly enough, the respondents' assessment of the factors' importance largely correlates with their identification of factors that limit Czech success in national interest promotion (correlation coefficient of 0.57, see Table 3.5). This suggests that the respondents do not highly regard the Czech performance in the EU, particularly in the factors that are key for the country's ability to shape EU decision-making.

The respondents offered additional factors for both questions on the factors important for Czech interest promotion and on factors that impede

Table 3.5 Correlation between which factors are considered important and which factors hinder Czech performance

	Total	Senior level	Working level	Foreign trade	ENP	Democracy and HR	CSDP
Correlation coefficient	0.57	0.37	0.61	0.28	0.36	0.89	0.43

better performance of the Czech Republic. Two main issues can be identified, suggested by several respondents independently. They highlighted the importance of predictable and consistent behaviour in the Council at all levels, including by the political representation of the country. Related to this is the need for active interest and participation of the Prague-based institutions as well as government members and parliamentarians in the European agenda. Several of the respondents insisted that the inability to define national interests that would be shared and supported by political elites hampered the Czech performance exactly by decreasing the predictability of Czech behaviour and by limiting the politicians' involvement in EU negotiations.

Human resources and their exploitation

As a closing question, the respondents were asked a binary question about their current job, namely whether they were at the moment working for the Czech administration on European issues. Academic literature suggests that learning is an important factor in increasing the effectiveness of interest promotion in the EU (Panke, 2010c: 813; see also Radaelli and Dunlop, 2013). Those who served in Brussels at the permanent representation have acquired extensive contacts in other member states as well as within the EU institutions. They have also deepened their understanding of how the Council and the rest of the EU decision-making process work well beyond the textbook descriptions. They are key for the state administration's learning process and valuable resources for the system's improvement.[8]

Given the importance of these officials' expertise, it is surprising to learn that out of the 30 respondents, only 12 claimed that they worked on the EU agenda for the Czech public administration. When those that were representing the Czech Republic in the Council at that time are removed from the list, the ratio is even more striking. In such a case, only 4 out of 22 respondents dealt with the EU agenda within the Czech public administration at the moment of filling in the questionnaire. In addition, this does not include those individuals whose contact details could not be acquired through their former colleagues or the ministry and did not have the chance to answer, so the real ratio would probably be even smaller than 4:18.

58 *Perceptions of Czech representatives*

There are no data available on where the respondents currently work. They may have remained in the Czech public administration, but deal with issues that are not related to the EU. They may also remain connected with the EU agenda, but have left the public administration for the private sector or EU institutions. Alternatively, they could have left both the area of expertise and the Czech public administration. Whichever of the scenarios is true, it does not make a difference from the perspective of the public administration's learning. The experience of the individuals that finished their jobs at the permanent representation does not contribute to Czech EU policy-making. As a result, it can be assumed that the Czech performance in the EU has been suboptimal, because the Czech Republic has not been able to build on the experience and expertise gathered through its EU membership as well as it could have.[9]

Summary of the chapter's findings and partial conclusions

The survey results provide for several tentative conclusions. In terms of the working hypotheses, the account is mixed. The data suggest that the Czech Republic's representatives use more methods of interest promotion the longer the country is an EU member. It thus supports the first working hypothesis, but the data seem to fluctuate a lot, and if the rookie year 2004 is added, the trend reverses.

The data offer more interesting and stronger results on the second and third working hypotheses, which take into account the lessons from the lobbying scholarship and classify the member state's efforts into three distinct categories: the methods focused on an individual dossier, the "early warning" methods, and methods for obtaining insider status. The data confirm the second hypothesis, albeit only partly. There is an apparent emphasis on "early warning" methods in the activity of Czech representatives in the Council. They use this type of methods most often at all levels and in all policy areas. Moreover, there seems to have been a revaluation of the respective methods' added value on the part of the Czech representatives, because the "early warning" methods used to be the least used in 2004. This finding fully corresponds with the theoretical expectations that consider early information key to successful interest promotion and suggest that the member states' representatives would use methods aimed at obtaining timely information more with longer membership.

In contrast, there is no significant increase in the use of methods that should provide the country with an insider status. In comparison with 2004, the occurrence of these methods has even slightly decreased. Two tentative and alternative explanations could make sense of this fact. First, the Czech representatives may not have understood yet that achieving an insider status is the easiest and most efficient way to promote their own interests in EU politics, or they have not been able to master the methods effectively enough to deliver results. Alternatively, the Czech representatives in the Council do not strive to become insiders on any policy issue because they are unable to prioritize and focus on key points on the agenda where they would have the chance to stand out. In such a case, it would not make sense to put effort into this type of methods and it would be more rational to focus on individual dossiers and obtaining early information. Indeed, the respondents suggest that the Czech performance in the EU is hampered by the inability to define national interests and rally around them both at the administrative and political levels. Such lack of prioritization renders any efforts to become an insider useless or even prevents the Czech representatives from applying some of the methods that would help them get into the inner circle of policy-shapers. In particular, ill-defined national interests make specialization and strengthening of expertise on key issues fairly impossible.

Turning to the third working hypothesis, there is no significant difference between the analysed policy areas. While it was expected that the negotiators would tend to use more sophisticated methods in areas where the EU institutions have more power and member states can be outvoted, this has not been confirmed by the data. In all policy areas the pattern seems to be the same: the activity is highest on "early warning" and relatively low on group 3, which is the most sophisticated group. In fact, group 1 and group 2 methods are most often used in foreign trade and in CSDP, which are the two most different areas, and group 3 methods are used most often in democracy and human rights policy and in foreign trade, which differ greatly in both the engagement of the institutions and the decision-making rules. At the same time, the Czech Republic tends to send more experienced diplomats to the working groups operating in a more "complex" environment with a more important role played by the institutions, such as foreign trade and ENP, and slightly less experienced diplomats to the working groups deciding by unanimity more often, such as those on diplomacy and human rights policy and on CSDP.

While the impact of the decision-making style and of the institutions' involvement has not been confirmed, the level of the working group and salience of the topic seems to matter a lot. First, all methods are used much more often at the senior level than at the working level. This could be explained by the fact that parts of the working level agenda are uncontroversial and do not require a lot of effort on the part of the negotiator. At the senior level, by contrast, the issues that could not be settled at the working level are negotiated. By definition, they contain a dispute among the member states and as a result, the negotiators need to be more active in order to secure a favourable result. The difference between the two levels of negotiation is reflected in the respondents' evaluation of how useful individual methods are to promote member states' positions or to block unwanted proposals. More exploratory methods are valued at the working level, such as consultations with the Commission or the presidency, whereas more bargaining and coalition-building methods are appreciated at the senior level, such as argumentation and reframing.

Second, the salience for Czech foreign policy of the topic on which the particular working group focuses seems to be important. The comparison between two geographical working groups within the scope of the ENP has revealed a significant difference. Where the focus of the working group overlaps with the Czech foreign policy orientation, i.e. the Eastern dimension of the ENP, the negotiators are more active, particularly when seeking timely information.

In general, the Czech representatives in the Council use methods that they consider effective and important for achieving success in the negotiations. This has been confirmed by the correlation between the perceived values of individual methods and the frequency with which the respondents put these methods into practice. The correlation coefficients are mostly positive, especially where there reach higher values. In addition, this claim is further supported by the fact that timely access to information is considered the most important factor for the Czech Republic's success in EU negotiations and at the same time, the group 2 methods that aim at granting the member state's representatives such timely access are most often used by the respondents.

The size of the member state (in terms of population and economy) seems to play an ambiguous role in the negotiations. On one hand, size is not considered important as a factor influencing the Czech ability to promote its interests, in particular at the senior level of negotiation and in some policy areas, such as democracy and human rights promotion. On the other hand, having the backing of one of the big member states is considered fairly important for successful promotion of the state's own proposals and crucial for blocking unwanted proposals. The Czech representatives' reading of the negotiation dynamics can thus be interpreted in the following way: very little can be pushed through against the active opposition of big member states, but that does not necessarily mean that the game is dominated and led by the big ones completely. Small member states can also promote their own interests successfully when they prepare well, such as by consulting informally with the institutions and other member states in advance, trading support, and using good arguments.

Probably the most striking finding concerns the Czech inability to look after its human capital. The Czech system seems to be unable to make use of the experience accumulated by the officials serving in Brussels, who in their vast majority do not contribute to the formulation of Czech EU policy upon their return from the permanent representation.

Notes

1 Observation and, particularly, participant observation could offer other insight, but are available only to a very limited group of researchers and potential researchers. In addition, they are often restricted to a single perspective determined by the observer's position in the system. They are, as a result, of limited use for a cross-policy and diachronic comparison.
2 After the April 2003 signature of the Accession Treaty, the representatives of the acceding states started participating in Council negotiations as observers.
3 Traditionally, the COHOM has been a working group whose members were based in their respective capitals permanently. Only recently was the working group

Perceptions of Czech representatives 61

restructured into two formations – the capital-based COHOM and the Brussels-based COHOM. Due to the centrality of democracy and human rights promotion in Czech foreign policy, however, the working group was included in the survey and the respective Czech representatives were asked to fill in the questionnaire, even though they may not have been placed in Brussels permanently. The Trade Policy Committee, in turn, is a relatively senior body to which a number of expert working groups report. These experts are, however, not placed in Brussels permanently. At the level of deputies, the Trade Policy Committee is the only trade-related body that has as broad an agenda as the working groups from other policy areas included in this research. In addition, there are two more senior levels in the Council structure to which the TPC at the level of deputies reports – the TPC at the level of full members and COREPER II. Therefore, the TPC is considered a working level group in this research.

4 The relatively high number of officials concluding their time in Brussels in 2009 can be explained by the fact that the permanent representation staff was boosted for the Czech Council presidency and returned to a normal level in 2009.
5 How experienced the diplomats in various working groups usually are may vary depending on policy area as well as practice in the Council. Mai'a K. Davis Cross (2010: 12) points out, for example, that while the EU Military Committee is staffed by three-star military officers, CivCom comprises officials at lower levels with a few exceptions only.
6 There can, naturally, be occasions when a member state is (due to a favourable context or other factors) able to secure its interests without any sophistication, but this cannot be expected to happen regularly.
7 The data in questions 8 and 9 have been adjusted in the following way: where the respondent included the extra option ("other") in the ranking, the option was taken out and the following answers' rank shifted upwards. In addition, where one or more of the answers was not assigned any value, they were considered the least important and assigned the value "1". In this way, the resulting data covering the eight predefined answers were homogeneous and allowed for further analysis.
8 Similarly important are the Czech nationals that have served in EU institutions directly, naturally.
9 The dismal work of human resources is further vindicated by the fact that the Foreign Ministry does not even maintain a list of individuals that have served at the permanent representation.

4 External trade

Reforming the Generalised System of Preferences[1]

Trade is one of the spheres where the European Union has been able to 'wield considerable influence' (Smith, 2011: 188). In fact, unlike other, more traditional powers, some authors consider the EU a 'trade power' (Meunier and Nicolaïdis, 2006) or a 'market power' (Damro, 2012), which captures the understanding of the EU as an actor that successfully influences others through the size of its market and through mutual trade relations. The EU is an active player in international trade negotiations both multilaterally and bilaterally, within international organizations, such as the WTO, and through concluding free trade agreements respectively (cf. Young and Peterson, 2014). Trade is also an important aspect of other EU external policies, notably development cooperation.

The Generalised System of Preferences (GSP) occupies a prominent position in the EU's trade relations with the developing countries. Being often too weak and vulnerable to match the developed countries' production on an equal footing, the developing countries are provided preferential access to the EU market both in terms of tariffs and quotas. The GSP principle arose from multilateral trade negotiations as an exception from the most favoured nation (MFN) clause of the General Agreement on Tariffs and Trade (GATT) in 1971 (for a history of the GSP, see Dos Santos et al., 2005; Shaffer and Apea, 2005). Under the GSP scheme, the recipients are given market access under more favourable conditions, i.e. lower tariffs, than developed countries at the MFN levels. This allows for marketing of the developing countries' products at more competitive price levels. The word "generalised" denotes the non-discriminatory basis of the GSP principle, which should cover developing countries disregarding their history and bind the developed countries not to favour their former colonies.

The European Union (European Community) established the Generalised System of Preferences for exports from developing countries in 1971. The system has undergone several reforms throughout the years that fine-tuned the levels of market access to different types of developing countries according to the development in the particular countries as well as the general political context. In the 1990s, for example, the EU established specific incentives arrangements within the general GSP to offer more advantageous market access to countries that advanced its labour, environmental, and anti-drug trafficking objectives (Council of the European Union, 1994; cf. Waer and Driessen, 1995). A major reform was induced by India's successful challenge of the EU's system at a WTO panel, which particularly targeted the discriminatory character of the anti-drug trafficking preference (Mathis, 2004; Shaffer and Apea, 2005).

As a result, the EU abolished some of the specific incentives and simplified the GSP system into three major arrangements of market access in 2005 (Council of the European Union, 2005). The standard scheme was available for all developing countries that were not classified as high-income countries by the World Bank for a certain period of time and had sufficiently diversified exports at the same time. Two specific schemes with more advantageous tariffs remained, but were conceived in such a way that inclusion relied on more objective factors than the challenged former anti-drug trafficking criterion. Moreover, they were open to all developing countries that fulfilled the criteria. First, the "GSP+" access was linked to ratification and implementation of the 16 core human and labour rights conventions of the United Nations and the International Labour Organization, and at least seven conventions related to environmental protection and good governance. Second, the least developed countries (LDCs) were offered an even more preferential scheme, in fact full duty-free and quota-free access, for all their exports with the exception of arms and armaments – the "Everything but Arms" arrangement (EBA).

Motivation and proposal for change

The new GSP system was considered successful in principle, but lacking effectiveness in several respects, such as the targeting of beneficiaries, the GSP graduation mechanism,[2] and the insufficient product coverage (cf. Gasiorek, 2010). In addition, the GSP was considered not to be sufficiently consistent with the overall EU trade and economic objectives (European Commission, 2011c). Therefore, the European Commission launched a new reform and presented a new draft regulation in 2011, which, while maintaining the three major lines of the GSP, aimed to address these deficiencies (European Commission, 2011f).

In general, the Commission was led by two overarching objectives in drafting the proposal. First, the GSP should better differentiate between developing countries and focus on those that really need the GSP preference to boost their development instead of those that enjoy the preference but would already be competitive without it. In order to do so, the Commission proposed a reduction of GSP beneficiaries. Besides the high-income countries, the upper-middle-income countries according to the World Bank classification for three consecutive years should no longer be eligible for preferential access. In addition, the developing countries that benefited from other comparable market access arrangements should also be considered non-eligible for GSP. As a result, the number of beneficiaries was expected to drop from 176 to around 80 (European Commission, 2011e).

64 *External trade*

Second, the GSP should not impede conclusion of bilateral trade agreements between the EU and other countries. Since the Commission's 2006 *Global Europe* communication, the EU had become the champion of trade liberalization (cf. European Commission, 2006b). This emphasis was reconfirmed by the 2010 communication *Trade, Growth and World Affairs* (cf. European Commission, 2010b). Given the stalemate of the Doha Round negotiations, the EU embarked on negotiating bilateral agreements with its trade partners all over the world, ranging from the Economic and Partnership Agreements with developing countries, such as the one concluded with the CARIFORUM states in 2008, to classic free trade agreements, such as the one concluded in 2010 with South Korea, to extensive treaties covering trade and investment, such as the ones recently concluded with Canada and negotiated with the United States (cf. De Ville and Orbie, 2011). A number of potential partners, however, had been benefiting from the GSP access and had little to gain from exchanging the GSP benefits for a new reciprocal trade agreement. By stripping them of the GSP access, the EU aimed to increase their willingness to conclude bilateral trade agreements in order to maintain access for their exporters at previous levels (Siles-Brügge, 2014).

Negotiation framework and results

The Commission tabled the proposal for a new regulation in May 2011 after a standard consultation procedure, which included the commissioning of an external analysis from the University of Sussex (Gasiorek, 2010). The Lisbon Treaty that had entered into force just a few months before prescribed the ordinary legislative procedure (OLP) for this particular regulation, which meant a qualified majority vote in the Council and approval by the European Parliament. The Council debated the dossier shortly in May 2011 and again in March 2012 and adopted the final draft as item A (without debate) in October 2012. The bulk of the negotiation was conducted within the Working Party on the Generalised System of Preferences (WP on GSP), which gathers officials travelling to Brussels from capitals, and also included the Trade Policy Committee at the level of both deputies and full members, although in a much more limited way (Interview #19). In the European Parliament, the dossier was debated in the Committee on International Trade (INTA), which held the primary responsibility and appointed the rapporteur, and the Committee on Development (DEVE). The draft regulation was adopted in the first reading in June 2012.

In principle, two main groups of states emerged in the Council, which, for the sake of simplification, could be labelled as "liberal" and "protectionist". The protectionist camp was ready to restrict the GSP access to the European market as much as possible in order to protect domestic producers; a particularly active member of this group was Portugal (Interview #21). The liberal camp, on the other hand, supported the Commission in preserving a relatively broad, but focused, GSP in principle, but its members were keen to review the list of countries that were about to be excluded from the scheme. This group included the United Kingdom, Spain, the Netherlands, and the Czech Republic. A significant number of member states, including most notably Germany, did not, however, openly support any of these like-minded groups and remained neutral in the debate. As a result, the two camps strived to create a blocking minority in the Council, because neither of them could realistically think of forming a qualified majority, and for obtaining concessions from the Commission and the rest of the member states (Interview #39). In the end, the two camps neutralized each other and the original draft was approved with very minor changes and Commission concessions (European Parliament and Council, 2012).

The procedural aspects of the draft became as important as its content, because the reform was the first proposal to be decided by the ordinary legislative procedure in the area of GSP (Interview #17). This had an impact on the planned implementation of the regulation, which anticipated that the Commission would amend the lists of beneficiaries through delegated acts. Unlike with implemented acts, where the member states are fully engaged through the comitology system, in the case of delegated acts it is the Commission alone that decides and the member states (and the European Parliament) are given a certain period of time to actively disagree only. The member states were rather unhappy about this loss of influence, but could not do much about it in the end, because the shift to delegated acts derived directly from the Treaty (Interview #39). In order to soften the impact on the member states and to ensure smoother implementation, the Commission committed itself to establishing an informal expert group with participation of officials from the member states and the INTA secretariat, which debates the draft delegated acts before they are sent into inter-service consultation and adopted by the College (Interview #18). This expert group has been in place ever since, usually convening once in two months (Interview #13).

The negotiations in the Council were relatively painful, with the liberal and protectionist camps blocking any progress for a long time. The Polish presidency did not manage to move the dossier forward in the second half of 2011, but the stalemate was successfully broken by the Danish presidency that followed. The Danish compromise proposal was very close to the original draft and managed to win the backing of a significant number of key actors, including Germany, as well as to persuade the two camps that no other option was available (Interview #39). At the same time, the careful compromise left very little room for the presidency to negotiate with the EP and the Commission in the trialogue, which was noted by the EP with annoyance (Interview #21).

The European Parliament welcomed the Commission proposal in principle. The parliamentarians favoured the reduction of the number GSP recipients and were keen to have more predictability in the GSP system, which was ensured by the ten-year validity of the proposed system. In addition, the MEPs paid attention to the GSP+ regime and supported more cooperation with civil society in evaluating the implementation of the international conventions in the beneficiary countries (Interview #21). Some MEPs clearly had their 'national hats on' (Interview #17) when debating the proposal. Similarly to the Council, however, the liberal and less liberal views neutralized each other and the parliament approved the draft smoothly in the first reading.

Czech interest and engagement in EU external trade

The Czech Republic is an open, export-driven economy, but most of its trade is directed to other EU countries. In 2012, about three-quarters of total turnover and about four-fifths of exports were produced in transactions within the EU (Czech Statistical Office, 2013). Moreover, the Czech Republic did not have a colonial empire in the past and does not have traditional ties to developing countries today. The total turnover of Czech trade with the developing countries amounts to just about 6 per cent of the total trade (Ministry of Industry and Trade of the Czech Republic, 2014).[3] It is therefore not surprising that the Czech Republic was never particularly active on GSP-related issues or even external trade issues in the past according to both its own negotiators and the EU institutions representatives (Interview #18; Interview #39). The bulk of its activity was directed towards internal market issues and energy policy where the Czech trade interests lie and where the Czech representatives have actively pursued further liberalization in both goods and services (Beneš and Braun, 2010: 65; cf. Government of the Czech Republic, 2009).

External trade is a sensitive area in institutional terms in the Czech context. The institution responsible for policy formulation is the Ministry of Industry and Trade (or Trade Ministry), but it has traditionally competed with and been assisted by the Ministry of Foreign Affairs (or Foreign Ministry), which engages in "economic diplomacy". The political demand for stronger economic diplomacy increased with the financial and economic crisis and so has the competition between the two ministries. At the moment, there are even two separate representation networks in support of trade: one run by the foreign ministry as part of regular embassies, the other run by the trade ministry under the label Czech Trade (Rubešková et al., 2014: 21).

Within EU policy-making, the situation bears some resemblance. The trade ministry is responsible for the formulation of the policy and its officials travel to Brussels to participate in various Council external trade working groups, including the WP on GSP. Also, the full member of the Trade Policy Committee is an official of the trade ministry at the level of deputy minister. It is, moreover, the Ministry of Industry and Trade that maintains contacts with the main associations of Czech exporters and importers and evaluates data on Czech trade within and beyond the EU. The Foreign Ministry also plays a role in the process, however. First, its officials take part in external trade negotiations at several important levels, including the COREPER (the permanent representative to the EU) and the Trade Policy Committee at the deputy level.[4] Second, there is a whole section dealing with economic issues at the Foreign Ministry, featuring, for example, the Department of Bilateral

Economic Relations and Export Promotion. This section not only comments on draft positions before they are adopted by the governmental Committee on the EU, but it also has the sole authority on some issues that are directly related to external trade and EU policy-making. In the area of GSP, for instance, it is the Foreign Ministry that is responsible for the oversight of the Commission's GSP+ evaluations on behalf of the Czech Republic. There thus needs to be working cooperation between the two ministries to both formulate and promote the Czech position in the EU negotiations.

Formulation of the Czech negotiation position

Relevant work on the Czech position began only after the proposal for the regulation was adopted by the Commission in May 2011. At that moment, the dossier arrived in the Department of Trade Policy and International Economic Organisations at the Ministry of Industry and Trade and was assigned to one of the officials (Interview #39). There is no information available about any significant Czech activity in the previous phases of the policy process, notably during the Commission's consultation and drafting phase.

The department decided to prepare an impact analysis of the proposed changes, which was drafted by the department officials. The analysis was based on statistical data and consultations with the ministry's territorial departments as well as with professional associations and academia (Interview #39). The study focused on the proposed changes in the list of GSP beneficiaries and aimed at identifying specific groups of products that were currently imported to the Czech Republic with the GSP tariffs and whose transfer to less advantageous tariff levels could have a negative impact on either Czech consumers or Czech industry. Most of the consequences were evaluated as marginal. The only exception was several groups of products imported as raw or partly processed materials from Russia and Kazakhstan that served as sources for Czech industrial production, such as ferro-chromium, methanol, and aluminium powders (Ministry of Industry and Trade of the Czech Republic, 2011).

The political demand from the incumbent leadership of the ministry and from the government was to present the Czech Republic as a liberal country in economic and external trade matters (Interview #16). During the first years after accession, the Czech Republic had been rather cautious and had tried to prevent negative impacts on domestic industry, parts of which had suffered during the transformation in the 1990s. The government, which was at that time led by the right-wing Civic Democratic Party, pushed for domestic liberalization and further liberalization of the EU internal market, and support for liberal approaches in external trade was a logical follow-up to these policies.

The Czech Republic has never been a particularly strong actor in EU development policy. In 2013, Czech official development assistance amounted to just 0.11 per cent of gross national income, which was well below the EU average (0.41 per cent) and did not, by far, meet the targets set for the Czech

Republic in the past (0.17 per cent) (European Commission, 2014). The Trade Ministry thus did not question the development-related objectives of the proposed regulation and accepted the bottom line of the Commission's argumentation about the necessity to reduce the number of GSP beneficiaries and focus on those most in need. At the same time, from the very beginning the Trade Ministry officials understood and supported the parallel effort of the Commission to increase pressure on third countries to conclude bilateral treaties with the EU (Interview #39).

As a result, the Czech policy in the GSP negotiation followed three basic lines. First, the Czech Republic supported the reduction of the list of GSP beneficiaries. Second, however, the GSP was to be maintained as a reasonable tool of EU development assistance and should not be reduced indefinitely. Finally, given the particular interests of Czech industry, the negotiators were supposed to push for a revision of the list of GSP eligible countries in order to return Russia and Kazakhstan to the list.

Czech activity during the negotiations

Having defined the priorities for the upcoming negotiations, the Czech negotiators set off to explore the positions of other member states and the distribution of votes in the Council with the aim to create a blocking minority that would force the Commission to adjust the draft in a favourable way (Interview #39). Given the ongoing debate in the WP on GSP, the other member states' priorities were collected from the formal interventions of their negotiators and from informal discussions on the WP's margin. It was obvious early on that three groups of countries had emerged in the Council: neutral countries that generally supported the Commission's proposal but were not very vocal during the negotiations, protectionist countries that wanted to cut the GSP as much as possible, and liberal countries that actively opposed the protectionists (as discussed above). Whereas the group of protectionist member states was rather well-organized and relatively unified in their objectives, the more liberal member states lacked a unified position, because each and every state was trying to secure a slightly different change to the original draft regulation.

The Czech officials aimed at reviewing the method of composing the list of GSP beneficiaries in order to return Russia and Kazakhstan to the list. The original draft relied on the World Bank evaluation of countries' incomes to distinguish between the rich and needy. Due to the WTO framework, it was necessary to maintain an "objective" basis for the list-making. Otherwise, the EU would have risked challenges at a WTO panel for discrimination. The Czech Republic proposed an additional criterion – the Human Development Index – to supplement the World Bank income ranking. According to this proposal, the upper-middle-income countries in the World Bank ranking would be stripped of their GSP access only when they were sufficiently developed according to the Human Development Index at the same time. Such an adjustment to the original proposal would, among others, ensure that both

Russia and Kazakhstan would retain their GSP benefits (unlike, for example, Brazil and Argentina). The Czech representatives were aware that such a proposal was most probably too ambitious and difficult to push through. However, they put it forward anyway as a maximal option from which they would be able to fall back to a still acceptable compromise, such as dropping Russia but keeping Kazakhstan on the list (Interview #16; Interview #39). Similarly, other liberal member states put forward their own additional criteria to return their pet countries to the list.

Understanding that the more liberal member states were finding themselves under pressure, the Czech diplomats made a bid for more efficient cooperation within the group. Representatives of the United Kingdom, the Netherlands, and Spain were invited for a breakfast at the Czech permanent representation where the opportunities for more coordinated cooperation were discussed. During this breakfast and the following meetings a common proposal was developed, which envisaged a single additional criterion of economic vulnerability, which used to be part of the GSP system, increased to 90 per cent. That would mean that the upper-middle-income countries would not lose their GSP access as long as 90 per cent of their exports to the EU were covered by the five largest sections of their export commodities (cf. UNCTAD, 2008: 13). A joint British–Czech non-paper to the Danish presidency was drafted containing the details of the suggested change. The common proposal was a compromise among the like-minded countries: the Czech Republic would not be able to keep the GSP benefits for Russia, but would preserve Kazakhstan. Spain, on the other hand, would not be able to shield Brazil or Argentina, but would maintain access for several other Latin American countries.

The joint proposal was a good compromise, but came too late to influence the negotiations in the Council. In the meantime, the Danish presidency had prepared its own proposal, which won the backing of the neutral countries, including Germany. In the end, the liberal coalition, although supported by several late newcomers, did not find the strength to block the adoption. Having realized that the cause was lost, some of the original like-minded group members did not even bother to speak up for the common proposal during the formal meeting of the WP on GSP (Interview #39). As a result, the Czech representatives accepted the Danish proposal and as a part of the package deal they achieved the establishment of a transition period of one year during which the GSP regime continued along the previous lines (cf. European Parliament and Council, 2012: Art. 41). That ensured that the Czech importers gained some time to find new business partners or to renegotiate the contracts with their Russian and Kazakh suppliers.

Besides the activity in the Council, the Czech negotiators tried to promote their cause in the European Parliament as well. Using the existing contacts between the permanent representation and Czech MEPs, the Czech position was delivered to all parliamentarians elected in the Czech Republic and more intensive cooperation was established with the only Czech MEP in the INTA committee. In the end, however, the MEP did not speak in the INTA debate on the dossier in December 2011 (European Parliament, 2011), nor did any of the Czech MEPs contribute to the final debate at the EP plenary in June 2012 (European Parliament, 2012). In fact, the vulnerability criterion does not feature anywhere in the EP documents on the dossier, hinting that the British–Czech proposal came too late to influence the results.

There were regular contacts between the Czech negotiators and a Czech Commission official close to the GSP dossier. The informal talks served as a source of information and check on the viability of the Czech arguments (Interview #16). The Czech official was, however, very cautious not to overstep the limits of the Commission's impartiality. Also given the advanced stage of negotiations, when the initiative was already to a large extent in the hands of the member states and particularly the presidency, such informal contacts could probably not have contributed much to the Czech argumentation.

Evaluation of the Czech engagement

Given the background of the suggestions put forward by the accounts on lobbying and advocacy, the most striking feature of the Czech engagement in the GSP reform is the fact that the Czech officials started working on the Czech position only when the draft regulation was revealed by the Commission. There had not been any significant engagement of the Czech Republic in the agenda-setting and policy-drafting phase of the policy process. The Czech endeavour was reactive with an attempt to forestall a disadvantageous policy that was already on the table, not an active contribution to the definition of objectives and policy options. It was, in fact, policy crisis management.

There are two alternative, but not mutually exclusive, explanations of this Czech reactive approach to the GSP reform. First, the Czech Republic is passive on external trade dossiers generally, as suggested by one of the interviewees. The country's negotiators formulate a position on the items on the agenda because they need to have a position in order to participate in the Council negotiations, but they do not have the political assignment, will, or capacity to shape the policy area more actively and contribute to agenda-setting. Alternatively, this might be just a case of a particular GSP dossier and relations with the developing countries in general, which do not belong to the most prominent Czech foreign policy interests.

Whether the former or the latter explanation be closer to the truth, the fact that the GSP regulation was identified by the stakeholders as the dossier where the Czech Republic invested a lot of effort in influencing the resulting policy suggests that policy crisis management is the default Czech activity in EU external trade negotiations. People acquainted with the Czech policy formulation and conduct on the GSP issue all agree that the unusually high level of Czech activity in this particular case was the result of the personal engagement of the desk officer in charge (Interview #13; Interview #16; Interview #18). Moreover, the desk officer's decision to put effort into this particular negotiation was supported by his superiors and a good working relationship developed between the representatives conducting the negotiations on behalf of the Czech Republic at all Council levels (Interview #16).

The lack of Czech ability to engage in EU external trade policy-making in the early phases of the policy process was not restricted to the state administration in this case. There was no significant activity from among the business stakeholders either. The ministry invited the Czech business sector to consultations and identified the potential impacts of the draft regulations, not the other way round. Apparently, if the ministry had not decided to conduct the consultations and to pen the impact analysis, the affected businesses would have simply found out about the higher price of their Russian and Kazakh supplies only when asked to pay more on import duties. Neither the affected companies nor their associations were able to identify the potential problems early in the process and call on the state to protect their interests.

The GSP case has shown that the Czech Republic is able to conduct standard negotiations in the Council. The Czech representatives understand the policy process well, they are able to identify the interests and blocs present in the negotiations and they know how to formulate a reasonable position and build a coalition. The Czech diplomats managed to gather a reasonable bloc of like-minded countries, which included influential member states, and to co-author a non-paper with the common position. The lack of success, i.e. the fact that both Russia and Kazakhstan were dropped from the list of GSP beneficiaries, to some extent was a result of the late activation of the like-minded group. From a bigger perspective, however, the Czech case was most probably lost from the very beginning and there was little opportunity to change the Commission's original proposal, which hit the balance between the liberals and the protectionists in the Council well.

Nevertheless, the Czech performance might have been more or less good in the Council, but it lacked the complexity and multifaceted nature that is the prerequisite of success in the EU. The Czechs clearly understand that the Council is different from other international negotiations and are able to negotiate informally with other member states and institutions as well as offer alternative solutions that fit into EU-style policy-making (contrast with Lempp, 2007: 36; Lewis, 2008: 176ff.), but this ability is limited to the Council only. At least in the GSP case, the Czech negotiators were unable to use informal contacts in the Commission and the European Parliament or other channels of influence to sway the decision-making. The bulk of the Czech attention remained focused on the Council.

There was probably little chance to influence the European Commission. That would have required engagement in the early phases of policy evaluation and drafting when the Czech Republic had not even had a defined position. The Czech Republic had been in an ideal position to gain background information in time, because there was a Czech official in the unit responsible for drafting the proposal personally known to the Czech officials at the Trade Ministry and the permanent representation. This information channel seems, however, not to have worked or at least it did not initiate any earlier activity from the Czech side.

72 External trade

The Czech negotiators were more active in targeting the European Parliament, but they were not successful. The Czech administration's system of engaging the European Parliament and the Czech MEPs in particular is still under development (Interview #12). As a result, the Czech administration and the Czech MEPs are not particularly good at working together in promoting the Czech interest. The GSP case shows this inability rather bluntly: the Trade Ministry identified the Czech interest and tried to contact the Czech MEPs, whose reaction was very limited and there was no trace of results in the Parliament's actual conduct whatsoever.

Notes

1 Substantial elements of this chapter were originally published in the article 'Too Limited, Too Late: Evaluating the Czech Republic's Performance as a Small-State Lobbyist in EU External Policy', *New Perspectives: Interdisciplinary Journal of Central and East European Politics and International Relations* 24(1), 2016. The article is available for download from the journal's blog – ceenewperspectives.iir.cz and more information about the journal can be found at newperspectives.iir.cz (cf. Weiss, 2016).
2 When a country becomes too rich or too successful in exporting some of its products to the EU compared to other GSP beneficiaries, it can no longer benefit from the preferential access either for any of its products (income graduation) or some of them (product graduation).
3 It should be noted, however, that the heading "Developing Countries" in the ministry's statistics includes neither the Commonwealth of Independent Nations (including Russia and Ukraine) nor "Others" (including China and Vietnam), which make up another 12 per cent of total trade combined. Some of these countries used to export their products to the EU in the GSP scheme.
4 The head of the Commercial Policy Section at the Czech permanent representation in Brussels, who is at the same time the member of the Trade Policy Committee at the level of deputies, is technically a Foreign Ministry official. He or she is, nevertheless, usually seconded from the Ministry of Industry and Trade.

5 European Neighbourhood Policy

Introducing the more-for-more principle to the European Neighbourhood Instrument

Being surrounded by a ring of stable and well-governed countries is of utmost importance for any country or bloc and the European Union is no exception. For a long time, the EU has searched for effective tools to help promote stability and good governance in its immediate neighbourhood. Whereas the Union based its influence in the neighbourhood mainly on the perspective of EU membership and the established enlargement policy until the early 2000s, there was a need to set up a new system of relations with the countries in Eastern Europe and the Southern Mediterranean that were not eligible for membership at all or could not be realistically expected to accede to the Union in the foreseeable future. The aim of the EU was to 'develop a zone of prosperity and a friendly neighbourhood – a "ring of friends" – with whom the EU enjoys close, peaceful and co-operative relations' (European Commission, 2003: 4).

The European Neighbourhood Policy (ENP) that emerged from this discussion as the main framework for the EU's relations with its immediate neighbourhood was largely modelled on the Union's experience with enlargement. Led by the Commission, the ENP is a collection of bilateral relations between the EU and the individual countries based on action plans and Commission evaluations. Having a thoroughly political objective of providing security and stability, it has, by and large, been a highly technical process of spending EU assistance money that has often provided few tangible incentives and avoided difficult issues, such as resolution of local and regional conflicts (cf. Nielsen and Vilson, 2014). From the beginning, it also suffered from the fact that it comprised a large number of countries that were incomparable in their development, problems, and aspirations, in particular the Southern and Eastern flanks. While the EU and its member states had a long history of relations with the countries of the Southern Mediterranean, including formalized fora such as the Euro-Mediterranean Partnership, also known as the Barcelona Process, the relations with the young states in Eastern Europe were newly institutionalized.

Two main obstacles have usually been mentioned when referring to the ENP: the bilateral character and the artificial bundling of the relations with the South and the East (cf. Cremona and Hillion, 2006). First, unlike in enlargement negotiations where the bilateral negotiation between the candidate state and the Commission is fundamental, the ENP concerned many issues that could not be solved between the individual state and the EU and required the cooperation of several countries in the region. Second, the Mediterranean and East European countries, while similar in several aspects, faced different challenges and expected very different things from their relations with the EU. As a result, the ENP was supplemented by two new initiatives in 2008 and 2009 respectively, the Union for the Mediterranean (UfM) and the Eastern Partnership (EaP).

Besides addressing the faults in ENP design by focusing on cross-border cooperation within the regions and adding an important civil society element, the two new initiatives recognized the different needs and contexts of the two neighbouring areas. They also reified the diverging interests of EU member states in the South that emphasized the involvement with the Arab countries and the states in the North and in Central Europe that considered the EU presence in Eastern Europe of vital importance. In addition, the almost parallel creation of the two frameworks ensured that the EU did not seem to prefer one of the regions and to abandon the other one (cf. Copsey and Pomorska, 2014).

Motivation and proposal for change

Since 2010 a large mid-term review of the European Neighbourhood Policy had been on the table, following the change of the Commission and on the basis of the evaluation of the first five years of the programme (European Commission, 2010a; Khalifa Isaac, 2013: 41; Tocci, 2011: 1). Overall, the Commission's evaluation of the ENP's progress was fairly positive, arguing that 'the EU [had] been able to establish a partnership for reform with its neighbours' that had 'brought tangible results benefiting both [the EU's] partners and the EU' (European Commission, 2010a: 14). At the same time, the Commission acknowledged that there had been deficiencies in implementation and that the ENP relies on the EU's ability to offer tangible benefits 'within a reasonable time frame' (European Commission, 2010a: 14), which was a criticism often brought forward by external experts (cf. Najšlová et al., 2013; Nielsen and Vilson, 2014; Wolczuk, 2009).

The ongoing revision was, however, interrupted by the Arab Spring events in early 2011 that pushed the EU to adopt earlier changes to the ENP, originally planned for the new budgetary period starting in 2014. The Arab Spring started in Tunisia with protests following the self-immolation of a street vendor, Mohamed Bouazizi, that led to the resignation and flight of Zine el-Abidine Ben Ali, the country's president of 23 years, in January 2011. Subsequently, popular protests started in a number of countries in the region. In some of them, the protests were minor or quickly suppressed by the governments. In others, however, they led to regime change, power struggles, and even to civil wars. The EU (and the West in general) was caught by surprise by the events that, on one hand, seemed to promote more democracy and, on the other hand, overthrew the EU's years-long partners and guarantors of stability. As a result, the EU sought for ways to incorporate more emphasis on democracy and good governance into the ENP documents and reformulate the ENP objectives to better reflect the popular demands and to strengthen the emerging democratic movements.

In spite of some authors' doubts about its novelty (Teti et al., 2013), the European Commission and the High Representative heralded a new approach to the Southern neighbourhood in the document titled *A Partnership for Democracy and Shared Prosperity with the Southern Mediterranean*, which was adopted in March 2011. This Partnership should be built on three elements: democratic transformation and institution-building, stronger partnership with civil society and opportunities for people-to-people contacts, and economic growth and development focused on small and medium enterprises, training and education, and poorer regions (European Commission and High Representative of the Union for Foreign Affairs and Security Policy, 2011a: 3). The idea was to boost the democratic movements in the region and to respond to the most pressing challenges that the Arab countries faced, namely the lack of institutions providing good governance and weak socio-economic development.

The core innovation or 'the fundamental step change' (European Commission and High Representative of the Union for Foreign Affairs and Security Policy, 2011a: 5) was the introduction of an incentive-based approach, in EU-speak referred to as the "more-for-more" principle. Departing from the existing practice when the financial assistance to the neighbourhood countries was distributed in advance, the more-for-more principle should guarantee more European assistance to states and societies that implement reforms faster and more thoroughly. The differentiated approach was later confirmed by the institutions in the May revision of the ENP and the concept of 'deep democracy' was introduced as the objective of the EU assistance (European Commission and High Representative of the Union for Foreign Affairs and Security Policy, 2011b; cf. Wetzel and Orbie, 2012 for the critique).

Given the fact that the main form of EU incentives to the neighbourhood had traditionally been financial assistance, it was necessary to translate the Union's willingness to support the democratic reform in the region and the differentiated approach in the set-up of financial allocations and financial instruments. The first opportunity came already in September 2011 when the Commission announced the establishment of the SPRING Programme (Support to Partnership, Reform and Inclusive Growth) that aimed at responding to 'the pressing socio-economic challenges ... of the southern Mediterranean' and to support those countries 'in their transition to democracy' (European Commission, 2011b). The programme was expected to distribute €350 million during 2011–2012 from the sources of the European Neighbourhood and Partnership Instrument (ENPI) – the standard financial tool of the ENP. Similarly, the more-for-more principle was introduced in the EU's assistance to the Eastern neighbourhood in the form of the EaPIC Programme (Eastern Partnership Integration and Cooperation) that was launched in June 2012 and planned to distribute €130 million, again from the ENPI budget (European Commission, 2012). The key confirmation of the altered approach to the reform processes in the neighbourhood, however, was to come with the debate on ENP financing for the next programming period 2014–2020 that started in early 2012 following the Commission's proposal of a regulation establishing a European Neighbourhood Instrument (ENI) in December 2011 (European Commission, 2011g).

Negotiation framework and results

The ENI negotiations were, if important, just one chapter in a longer debate over the overall course of the European Neighbourhood Policy. Traditionally, the EU member states had differing priorities in the neighbourhood with the Southern states, such as France and other Club Med countries, focusing more on the Mediterranean, and the Northern and Central European countries, such as Sweden and Poland, prioritizing Eastern Europe.

Over the years, two cleavages developed in the ENP debates that were both connected to the geographical priorities. First, there was a debate about relative financial allocations, which had resulted in the distribution of funds between the South and the East in a 2:1 ratio (cf. Bloomfield et al., 2011: 41). This had, however, never been put down on paper formally, which offered the EU member states the opportunity to try to tip the balance in favour of their preferred region in each budgetary discussion. Second, there has traditionally been an argument between the proponents of development and democratization assistance in the EU, with the first group emphasizing the socioeconomic development of the target countries and the second putting emphasis on democracy and rule of law (cf. Youngs, 2001). Whereas this cleavage is generally debated as the first and second generation of a human rights problem (cf. Tomuschat, 2008: 3), in the EU context it brings about important policy implications. The focus on democracy and rule of law distributes the EU assistance more or less equally and all countries in the neighbourhood are eligible for receiving EU money. The socioeconomic development criterion, on the other hand, favours the populous and underdeveloped South at the expense of the East.

The two main points of debate in the ENI negotiations reflected these two cleavages among the EU member states. The first contested issue revolved around the translation of the more-for-more principle into the ENI regulation. Traditionally, the ENP instrument distributed in advance the total amounts that individual target countries could receive. That allowed for better predictability and planning, but did not enable flexible reaction to current developments. Also, the system was incompatible with the more-for-more principle that was supposed to contribute more to those that reform, because the maximum limits were fixed in advance. The Commission's original proposal reflected this need by stipulating that financial allocations 'shall be determined using transparent and objective criteria reflecting the differentiation principle' (European Commission, 2011g, Art. 7 para. 5). It did not, however, specify how exactly the differentiation should be done and whether there would be any limits to the reshuffling of the money depending on the target country's performance. The Council debate centred exactly on whether such a "*fourchette*", constituting a 'dedicated performance reserve' (European Commission, 2011d: 24), should be set in the regulation and if yes, how big it should be. A higher *fourchette* could both increase the conditionality of EU assistance and destabilize the 2:1 distribution of funds, so it was promoted by those member states that concentrated on the political significance of the ENP, rather than the developmental needs of the receiving countries. In addition, a similar discussion accompanied the so-called "umbrella", the multi-country programmes that also made the exact funding available for each target country depending on their reform efforts uncertain.

The second contested issue concerned the criteria according to which the countries would be deemed as doing "more" reform and thus as being eligible to receive "more" funding. In line with previous debates on how to react to the Arab Spring, some member states preferred to keep the focus strictly on democracy and political rights whereas others wanted to expand the evaluation to cover socioeconomic reforms too. Broadening the criteria would make it easier for target countries to score on reform enthusiasm, thus limiting the impact of the conditionality measures in the ENI (Interview #27). In addition, it was unclear how the individual countries' progress should be evaluated and by whom.

The regulation was disputed not only among the member states in the Council, but also among and within the institutions. The EEAS understood more-for-more as a foreign policy tool where it is less important how much money is spent where than what type of political gesture the EU makes by assigning or not assigning the extra funds (Interview #35). Similarly, the Commissioner and his secretariat were keen to see more-for-more firmly established in the ENI regulation, although they had different views on the size of the *fourchette* than some of the more active member states (Interview #32). The DG DEVCO, in contrast, was concerned with the practicalities of the implementation and saw more-for-more as a liability in terms of predictability of aid, long-term planning, and absorption capacity of the target countries (Interview #27; Interview #34).

The negotiations were going on in the Council during the whole first half of 2012, but the difficult issues, in particular the question of whether the *fourchette* should be included and how big it should be, were put off by the opponents of the whole concept (Interview #44). It therefore came as a surprise to all when the Commission published its regular report on the ENP in May 2012 containing an evaluation of the neighbourhood countries according to the more-for-more principle (European Commission and High Representative of the Union for Foreign Affairs and Security Policy, 2012a: 3–4). Not only was the evaluation based on criteria that had not been explained to anybody, but it was even made without the knowledge of the comitology structures attached to the ENPI (Interview #44). The report clearly showed that the institutions expected the more-for-more principle to remain part of the ENP funding and, moreover, that they planned to be in charge of the process of evaluation and rewarding. The member states held their positions at the expert level and were unable to find a viable compromise for a long time. The issue even entered the agenda of COREPER II several times where the ambassadors bargained on the concrete numbers and allocations. In the end, a compromise was found at the level of ambassadors and the Council adopted a partial general approach on the ENI as an item A (without debate) on 25 June 2012. The European Parliament approved the draft regulation with amendments reflecting the Council compromise in December 2013 (European Parliament, 2013a). The Commission and the Council duly accepted the Parliament's amendments and the regulation was signed into law on 11 March 2014.

The final text of the regulation, in the end, endorsed the differentiated approach and the more-for-more principle by introducing both the umbrella and the *fourchette* adjustments to the ENI budget (European Parliament and Council, 2014a). The *fourchette* amounts to 10 per cent of the total ENI budget and the actual allocations are supposed to be decided 'on the basis of progress towards deep and sustainable democracy and implementation of agreed reform objectives contributing to the attainment of that goal' (Art. 7 para 6). It is the Commission that decides who gets the extra allocation and how much, on the basis of the regular evaluations by the EEAS (Interview #27). As a concession to the member states opposing the introduction of the more-for-more principle, the regulations stipulate that the country allocations should be determined on the basis of 'transparent and objective criteria' (Art. 7 para. 4), thus increasing the predictability of the assistance and limiting the availability of the instrument as a political tool. The regulation is, however, vague on what exactly these objective criteria should be.

Czech interest and engagement in the European Neighbourhood Policy

Being a smaller member state with limited foreign policy capacities and foreign policy history, the priorities of Czech external action were traditionally focused on the immediate neighbours. In the 1990s and early 2000s, the Czech Republic focused on settling its relations with Germany and Austria in particular (cf. Handl, 2009; Šepták, 2009). In addition, ties to the United States and key West European countries were considered crucial for the country's aspirations for NATO and EU membership. With the aim to reassert its "Western" and "European" credentials, the Czech Republic aligned with EU foreign policy declarations and actively contributed to NATO crisis management missions in the Balkans. After the accession, the Czechs quickly declared their support for further EU enlargement, which became one of the main issues promoted at the EU level and featured in the domestic debate about the EU as well, for example as an argument for Lisbon Treaty ratification (cf. Topolánek, 2009). By extension, the support to enlargement has embraced the European Neighbourhood Policy too, in particular its Eastern dimension (Weiss, 2015a). It was considered an important tool to engage countries that did not have a realistic short-term perspective of EU membership.

Apart from the geographical focus and under the influence of former dissidents that entered the diplomatic corps, Czech foreign policy incorporated support for human rights and democracy as "principles" of its external action (Government of the Czech Republic, 1999, 2003). These principles informed not only the general approaches, but resulted in concrete policies implemented by a newly established specialized Department for Human Rights and Transition Promotion Policy at the Foreign Ministry in 2005 (cf. Bartovic, 2008). The "transition policy" funds and supports activities in selected target countries focusing on issues of civil society and civil rights defenders, media and access to information, rule of law and good governance, election processes, and equality and non-discrimination (Ministry of Foreign Affairs, 2010).

In the ENP framework, Czech foreign policy focused ever more on relations with the post-Soviet countries in Eastern Europe at the expense of relations with the South, where only Israel was considered an important partner. The Czech EU Council presidency in 2009 happily supported the Polish–Swedish Eastern Partnership initiative, which was considered a well-designed tool to engage the Eastern Europeans not fit for EU membership, ensure good relations with oil and gas transit countries, and rebalance the ENP after the launch of the UfM the year before (Placák, 2010). In addition, the Czech policy could draw on the country's past and build on its 'own historical experience with a non-democratic regime and the process of political and economic transformation' in its support to transition in the post-Soviet states much more than in the Southern Mediterranean with its different history (Office of the Deputy Prime Minister, 2007; cf. Weiss, 2011 for the debate on identity and solidarity in Czech policy towards Eastern Europe).

In institutional terms, the Czech engagement in the ENP is managed by the Ministry of Foreign Affairs. Due to the complexity of the ENP, both in terms of issues and geographic scope, there are a number of departments at the ministry that are involved in ENP matters, such as the North and East Europe Department, the Middle East and North Africa Department, the CSFP Department, the Department for Human Rights and Transition Promotion Policy, as well as the horizontal EU departments responsible for cross-cutting issues. Moreover, the ministry has appointed a special envoy for the Eastern Partnership who is directly subordinated to the first deputy minister. Similarly, at the permanent representation in Brussels, multiple officials deal with the ENP, namely the representatives to the COEST and MaMa working parties and, naturally, the ambassadors in the PSC and COREPER II. Unlike at the permanent representations of bigger member states, there is always just one person responsible for the respective working parties in the Czech case.

Formulation of the Czech negotiation position

Given the long-term focus on human rights and transition to democracy in combination with the predominant interest in Eastern Europe, it is not surprising that the Czech Republic belonged, without any hesitation, to the group of states that supported a bigger *fourchette* oriented solely to democratic reforms. In fact, the Czech engagement in ENP reform had started before the events of the Arab Spring made changes to the scheme inevitable. In particular, the Czechs kept questioning the 2:1 South to East ratio that they considered too rigid and an obstacle to the EU's effective reaction to the developments in the neighbourhood (Interview #44). At the same time, they never pushed too hard on the issue, because the Commission seemed to be too keen on this informal principle and, in addition, they feared that any change could leave the East even worse off (Interview #22). For the same reason, the Czechs quickly abandoned the idea of pushing for the separation of East and South financing in the ENI.

There was, therefore, a need for a paradigm change. Instead of raising the issue of the sacred ratio, the Czech diplomats decided to include the issue of merit in the debate in the EU (Interview #24). This resulted in a letter by Minister Schwarzenberg in September 2010, which proposed 'differentiated and selective integration' of the ENP countries (Interview #44). Either the letter served as direct inspiration or it just resonated with ideas already being discussed in the Commission and the emerging EEAS; in any case the differentiated approach, in the form of more-for-more, became the centre point of the institutions' reaction to the Arab Spring in the following year.[1] What remained unclear, however, were the specific criteria that should serve as the trigger for more assistance. The Czech Republic supported the narrower democracy-based criteria, leaving out the socioeconomic development.

The formulation of the negotiating position was the sole responsibility of the Ministry of Foreign Affairs during the period in question. Other sectors had the opportunity to influence the Czech stance through the governmental EU committee, but they were not interested in ENP matters and gave the Foreign Ministry a free hand (Interview #24). Similarly, business did not pay much attention to the ongoing negotiations; they were interested in how to gain access to the opportunities created by the EU's funds for the neighbourhood, less so in where and by which principles these funds were distributed (Interview #44). The involvement of think tanks and academic experts was and had been more complex. The Czech Republic had traditionally presented itself as an EU member state with interest and expertise in the East European region. The Czech NGOs and policy institutes have, indeed, been active in Eastern Europe, not least encouraged by the Czech transition assistance (Najšlová, 2013; cf. Weiss, 2015a). In the case of more-for-more and ENI negotiations, the Czech officials responsible were acquainted with the publications of these institutions and some of them, namely the NGO platforms on development and transition policy, FORS and DEMAS, were even directly consulted on more-for-more (Interview #44). This was, however, rather an exception than a rule, because there had always been a problem in connecting this type of expertise with policy-making, both at the level of politicians and ministry officials (Interview #22).

Czech activity during the negotiations

It has already been mentioned that the Czechs had tried to influence the shape of ENP reform before the Arab Spring and the emergence of the more-for-more debate. One of the first occasions for the different opinion groups to crystallize was during early 2010 when France invited High Representative Ashton and Commissioner Füle to fix the 2:1 South to East ratio officially. A like-minded group led by the United Kingdom with the participation of the Czech Republic, Germany, and Poland, among others, was formed to discourage the institutions from doing so (Interview #44). This group was brought back to life in early 2012 during the ENI negotiations to lobby in the institutions for more conditionality in the ENP funding and to face a similar traditional like-minded group of Club Med countries led by France that saw the conditionality and more-for-more principle as a threat to the distribution ratio (Interview #37).

According to the Czech officials, the Czech Republic played an important role in the like-minded group where it was a member. This was possible thanks to very detailed positions that the Brussels-based representatives were receiving from the ministry and the interest and personal engagement of the ministry leadership that contributed to the negotiations at their respective levels (Interview #41; Interview #44). It is difficult to assess how important this role was, however, because when asked directly for their evaluation of the Czech engagement, officials from the institutions do not mention the Czechs among the most active member states in the ENI negotiation (Interview #26; Interview #27; Interview #32).

The Czech position profited, without any doubts, from the fact that the responsible commissioner, Štefan Füle, was nominated to the Commission by the Czech Republic. This advantage was, however, more related to the perceived strength of the Czech representatives rather than based on a real ability to influence the Commission's position and agenda. There were regular informal meetings that helped the Czech Foreign Ministry representatives get first-hand information about the commissioner's views and plans (Interview #11; Interview #24). According to several senior officials at the Czech Foreign Ministry, however, the commissioner's decisions were primarily motivated by his own agenda that did not always overlap with the Czech preferences (Interview #22; Interview #24). At the same time, the commissioner's nationality did improve the Czech reputation among other EU members and especially among the East European partners who 'did not believe that Füle did not follow our [the ministry's] instructions' (Interview #22; Interview #44).

Similarly, the role of the Visegrád Group, whose members all supported more conditionality in ENI, was recognized by the institutions, but was not considered crucial (Interview #32). At the same time, Visegrád cooperation has been well recognized in the Eastern ENP countries and as such might have helped the Czech Republic to raise its profile on the ENP in general (Interview #22). It should probably be mentioned in this context that the European Parliament's rapporteur on the ENI dossier was Eduard Kukan, former foreign minister of Slovakia, a V4 member.

The Czech engagement was clearly held back by insufficient capacities during the ENI negotiations. There was a single official responsible for the EU instruments at the Foreign Ministry who prepared the Czech positions and one official negotiating in Brussels at the working group level. The Brussels-based official was, however, responsible for the whole COEST agenda at the same time, which was far broader and richer than just the financial issues. In contrast, the British representative who played a leading role in the like-minded group that favoured more conditionality was responsible for the ENI negotiations only (Interview #41). During the last phases of the negotiations when the issue was debated by COREPER several times and the question concentrated on the exact size of the individual parts of the ENI (country envelopes, umbrella programmes, the *fourchette*), the Czech officials were backed significantly by their superiors at the ministry. Direct phone calls between the capitals focused on exchange of support on concrete formulations and amounts both within the like-minded group and beyond (Interview #44). The bargaining was possible because the ENI was a complex instrument with many issues to make a deal with and the Czech Republic had a clear and detailed position on many of them (Interview #41).

The Czech activity was much lower in the following phases of the evolution of ENI regulation. The compromise made among the member states in the Council was so difficult and so delicate that the other institutions confirmed it without significant adaptations. The compromise, which endorsed more conditionality based on democratic reform in the target countries, also was in line with the prevalent opinion in the European Parliament and the commissioner's cabinet (Interview #27; Interview #32).

Evaluation of the Czech engagement

Czech representatives have considered the result of the ENI negotiations a success (Interview #44). The regulation confirmed the introduction of the more-for-more principle into the ENP and based the evaluation of progress firmly on democracy-related criteria. The Czech Republic may have shifted its preferences in the neighbourhood since 2012, mainly because of the crisis in Ukraine, change of course in Armenia, and political instability in Moldova, which, among other consequences, may cause Eastern Europe to lose money as a result of the more-for-more principle.[2] In 2012, however, the result of the negotiations clearly satisfied Czech needs: the fixed 2:1 South to East ratio was undermined by the introduction of the *fourchette* and the umbrella programmes, and evaluation on the basis of simpler and broader socioeconomic criteria was avoided.

The Czech negotiators were in an advantageous position because they had a good source of timely information (the commissioner and his cabinet) and the negotiations touched upon an issue that had been a long-term priority of Czech foreign policy. In addition, the ENI negotiation was just a third act of the process that had already begun in 2010 with the French attempt to fix the 2:1 ratio and continued in 2011 with the EU's reaction to the Arab Spring. Nonetheless, the ministry was 'shocked' by the speed with which other member states, notably France, could react to the Arab Spring and tilt the ENP towards the South (Interview #44).

The ENI debate was notable due to the extensive use of reframing and introduction of positive concepts by both groups of member states to promote their positions. While the Czech Republic was clearly unhappy with the 2:1 ratio in the distribution of the ENP funding, these numbers were never raised in the discussion. Instead, the respective like-minded group argued for more "conditionality" and "flexibility" in the ENP. In contrast, the French-led group of states that opposed the introduction of the more-for-more principle put forward the argument of better "predictability" of EU assistance and concentration on "recipient countries' needs", even though their main motivation could have been the protection of the ratio in which the money was distributed.

The fact that the Czech representatives could 'get in touch with high politics' (Interview #44) on the ENI dossier is a result of the combination of a detailed and carefully prepared negotiating position, personal dedication of the responsible officials in Prague and Brussels, and a strong political mandate and backing, which was facilitated by the Czech perceived co-responsibility for the future of the Eastern Partnership that had been launched during the country's Council presidency. What naturally helped was the fact that the Commission, and particularly the commissioner, favoured the introduction of more-for-more and that both the commissioner's cabinet and the European Parliament supported the restriction of the evaluation criteria to democratic reform. In addition, the Czech representatives cooperated well with the bigger member states, notably the United Kingdom, which led the like-minded group informally, and Germany. This has been the established Czech practice in the ENP domain: to offer an idea to a stronger actor, usually Poland or Germany, and support their proposal (Interview #22).

On the other hand, the Czech Republic was not able to use other channels of influence that could have made the promotion of its position more effective. Most importantly, it did not try to affect the reporting to the institutions from the EU delegations in the ENP countries. These reports, including the so-called HoMs' reports that are result of the joint work of all EU heads of missions in the respective country, constituted an important input in forming the proposal by the Commission and the EEAS (Interview #35). The Czech representatives had been aware of this deficiency for some time, but had not been able to improve the performance in this area. The Czech embassies were asked to feed in their opinion on ENP reform as early as in 2010, but that was where their involvement ended (Interview #22; Interview #44).

To sum up, the Czech Republic was, or at least attempted to be, an active agenda-setter on the issue of ENP reform and the introduction of the more-for-more principle. Although it was forced to react quickly to others' unexpected proposals on occasion, most of the time it had a clear and detailed idea about what should be achieved and why. It had timely information and was able to maintain coherence at the working and political levels. Moreover, it was able to contribute actively to the negotiations within and beyond the like-minded group and to use its connection with the bigger member states to promote its cause. While the context was particularly favourable for an ENP reform, which contributed to the final positive result of the Czech endeavour without any doubts, the negotiations over ENP reform and the ENI regulation have shown that the Czech Republic is able to use a wide spectrum of tools to promote its interest in the European Neighbourhood Policy.

Notes

1 While some at the Czech Foreign Ministry believe that the Czech Republic was the original author of the more-for-more idea (Interview #22), the general understanding in the institutions is that the concept was developed within the institutions (Interview #26; Interview #27; Interview #32; Interview #35).
2 There has been a general trend at the Foreign Ministry to reach out beyond the issues of direct interest to the Czech Republic in order to play a more responsible role in EU external affairs and have more influence as a result. This was demonstrated by the Czech decision to contribute to the CSDP mission in Mali in 2013. In the ENP area this can be documented by significant resources committed to Egypt in the Czech transition policy budget as well as renewed debate at the ministry about the establishment of a special envoy for the Southern Mediterranean to "balance" the already existing special envoy for the Eastern Partnership.

6 Democracy and human rights
Implementing the recommendations of EU Election Observation Missions

Democracy and respect for human rights belong to the founding values of the European Union (Art. 2 TEU), which the EU aims to promote (Art. 3 TEU). The way in which norms inform EU behaviour have led some scholars to specific interpretations of the EU's identity in international relations, labelling the EU a 'normative power' (Manners, 2002). Many of the basic values in Article 2 of the Treaty on European Union feed into the general principles that the EU claims to observe in foreign affairs, but have not been institutionalized into a single budget line, with the exception of democracy and human rights.

While the European Community started supporting democracy in the mid-1980s, the assistance was institutionalized in 1994 with the establishment of the European Initiative for Democracy and Human Rights, which became the European Instrument for Democracy and Human Rights (EIDHR) in 2006 (Smith, 2007). The EIDHR is a specific instrument in which the rules follow the substance. Unlike other instruments of foreign assistance that primarily offer support to programmes organized by the governments of the target states, such as the European Neighbourhood Instrument (ENI) or the Instrument of Pre-accession Assistance (IPA), the EIDHR is meant to support democracy and human rights in countries that lack both and as a result, the projects often need to be conducted without the consent or even knowledge of local governments. This is reflected in the somewhat more flexible rules for project approval and financing (Lovitt and Řiháčková, 2008). Political considerations are always part of the EIDHR programming and implementation, because the projects supported by the instrument are clearly political and may annoy regimes that otherwise could be important partners for the EU or some member states' governments. This stands in stark contrast to the traditional instruments of foreign assistance, such as the ENI, IPA or the Development Cooperation Instrument, that in the vast majority focus on long-term apolitical, or at least less political projects.

One of the less controversial points of focus for the EIDHR has been the funding of EU Election Observation Missions (EOMs). Elections are, according to the European Commission, not equal to democracy, 'but they are an essential step in the democratisation process and an important element in the full enjoyment of a wide range of human rights' (European Commission, 2000: 4). Election observation is not specific to the EU. In fact, a large number of international governmental and non-governmental organizations observe elections and this has also been recognized at the UN level where the practice has been broadly defined and its objectives identified (United Nations, 2005). Traditionally, electoral observation has been the domain of the Organization for Security and Co-operation in Europe (OSCE), whose member states have committed to accepting observers from fellow member states (OSCE, 1999: 25) and which has a specialized office, the Office for Democratic Institutions and Human Rights (ODIHR) that is considered an important authority in EOM methodology (cf. OSCE, 2010). A number of other international organizations have participated in electoral observation, however, including the African Union, the Organization of American States, and the Commonwealth. The EOMs have also attracted the attention of political science and international relations scholars who focus mainly on the impact of the missions on the internal situation in the host countries, the mutual relations between the host countries and the countries and organizations sending out observers, as well as on the conceptual and organizational weak spots of the missions (cf. Carothers, 1997; Fawn, 2006; Kelley, 2009, 2010; Meyer-Resende, 2006; Milward, 2011).

The EU entered the field of election observation in 1993 with an EOM during the elections to Russian Duma. Since then, the EU has organized more than 150 missions all over the world (Kocsis, 2015: 101). Given the fact that all EU member states are at the same time members of the OSCE, the two organizations have established an informal division of labour with the OSCE monitoring elections in its member states and the EU sending its monitors beyond the OSCE area (Milward, 2011: 31). Most of the EU EOMs are therefore deployed in Africa, Latin America, and South East Asia (cf. EEAS, 2015a). The EU EOMs have developed into a well-established example of 'unique inter-institutional coordination' in EU foreign policy (Interview #51). All major EU institutions participate in the preparation and conduct of the missions: the EEAS and the Council decide on where to send the missions, the Commission pays for their deployment, the chief observer is always a member of the European Parliament, and the observers are sent out by the member states. The EU has been constantly developing and refining its own EOM methodology (European Commission, 2006a, 2008) both in the dialogue within the institutions and beyond, through financing specific NGO-run projects, such as the Election Observation and Democratic Support (EODS) project.

The EOMs are but a part of the EU's attention to democratic elections worldwide. Beside the observation missions that supervise the actual conduct of elections and evaluate how "free and fair" they were, including issuing recommendations on what should be improved to make the elections freer and fairer, the EU also invests significant money into election assistance. Election assistance consists of support to reforms that should contribute to more democratic elections, such as the work of electoral commissions and registration of voters (European Commission, 2000).

Motivation and proposal for change

Unlike in other case studies in this book, the issue of the EOMs' recommendations within the area of EU support to human rights and democracy cannot be simply reduced to a single decision by the European Union. The European support to human rights and democracy has been developing over time with parts of the policy being defined by individual decisions and parts resulting from the actual practice of EU institutions. The case of Election Observation Missions is a case in point, because their implementation depends on a number of factors from regulations that set the size of the budget to coordination practice among the EU institutions to informal methodologies developed for the EU by external actors.

There was a clear understanding among the EU institutions, the member states, and the policy practitioners that the EU was underperforming with regard to support to democratic elections in its target countries in the early 2010s. On one hand, the EU had growing expertise in conducting the observation missions and invested large amounts of money in electoral assistance. On the other hand, there was insufficient coordination of the various instruments and tools that the EU had at its disposal to support free and fair elections worldwide and lack of coordination between them. Particularly, the EU had been criticized for not being able to follow up on its own missions' recommendations by experts and practitioners alike who pointed out that the EU EOMs often produced recommendations that just repeated what the previous missions had suggested (cf. Meyer-Resende, 2006; Interview #52; Interview #54). The lack of systematic follow-up on the EOMs' reports was acknowledged by the EU institutions and highlighted in the Council's EU Action Plan on Human Rights and Democracy in June 2012 as well as in the Joint Report by the Commission and High Representative on Democracy Support in the EU's External Relations later in the same year (Council of the European Union, 2012; European Commission and High Representative of the Union for Foreign Affairs and Security Policy, 2012b).

In 2013, the preparation of the new EU multi-annual financial framework for the years 2014–2020, which included reconsideration and reprogramming of the main financial instruments, offered an opportunity to strengthen the role of the EOMs and their recommendations for EU external action. Among others, the EIDHR regulation was also subject to negotiation, which meant that not only the size of the EIDHR budget was to be decided, but also the whole structure of the instrument's support could be rebuilt. The EIDHR regulation forms the basic framework, which is refined by multi-annual indicative programmes and further by annual action programmes. A change can thus occur at various levels and in different moments of policy-shaping: radical restructuring requires an adjustment of the regulation, lesser but still significant changes need to be reflected in the multi-annual indicative programme, and minor adjustments can materialize in annual action programmes only.

The Commission proposed the draft EIDHR regulation in December 2011, after a public consultation and as a part of a series of draft regulations on external action instruments for the period 2014–2020 (European Commission, 2011h). While confirming the need for a specific instrument funding human rights and democracy in the world, the Commission proposed to increase the size of the overall EIDHR budget from €1.10 billion euro (for the previous period 2007–2013) to €1.58 billion. The instrument was found to be well designed and as a result, the Commission did not propose any major change to the focus and priorities of the EIDHR. At the same time, a 'better enabling regulation' should allow for quicker, better integrated, and more targeted reaction by the EU, including a 'better integrated approach to democratic cycles' that should combine 'election observation and other types of support to democratic and electoral processes' (European Commission, 2011h: 5–6).

At the same time, the Commission continued to support processes that led to fine-tuning of the election observation methodology and the general quality of the EU's democracy support focused on elections. While the projects implemented by NGOs and funded by the EU from the EIDHR budget, such as the Network for Enhanced Electoral and Democratic Support (running from 2001 to 2012) and the Election Observation and Democratic Support project (running since 2013), have no impact on the text of the EIDHR regulation, its priorities, and the size of the budget, they influence the "softer" rules that guide the EU's performance in electoral observation and contribute to adjusting its methodology. The ongoing dialogue between the Commission's DG DEVCO, the EEAS, the member states, and the NGOs active in election observation further pushed for adjustments of the EU's practice in implementing the general guidelines proposed by the draft EIDHR regulation.

Negotiation framework and results

Given the dual character of EIDHR programming through the EIDHR regulation and the subsequent multi-annual and annual programmes, the negotiation on EU electoral observation and support occurred on various levels with the participation of various actors with different roles. In the case of the EIDHR regulation, for example, the basic treaties prescribe adoption by the ordinary legislative procedure, which means approval by qualified majority in the Council and agreement by the European Parliament. The multi-annual and annual programmes, in contrast, are implementing acts and as such they are subject to an examination procedure by a specific committee established by the EIDHR regulation.

Although the draft regulation had already been sent over to the Council and the Parliament in December 2011, the bulk of the negotiations took place over summer 2013 only. In the Council, the draft regulation was discussed over some ten regular and extraordinary meetings of the Human Rights Working Group (COHOM) (Interview #49). As it was possible to find a compromise at the working level, the senior political bodies, notably the Political and Security Committee, did not have to enter the discussion at all (Interview #53). The proposal was not found problematic in the European Parliament either and, as a result, it was adopted, with amendments agreed to by both the Council and the Commission, in the first reading in December 2013 (European Parliament, 2013b).[1] The regulation was signed into law in March 2014.

During the negotiations, the member states' representatives in COHOM focused on two major issues in relation to election observation. First, there was a debate about whether a fixed part of the EIDHR budget should be predetermined to fund election observation missions, which had been the practice in the previous financial period. Second, there was the question of the EOMs' follow-up and how strongly it would feature in the text of the regulation. The earmarking of part of the EIDHR budget for election observation proved to be the more controversial issue among the two and the negotiators spent about four times more time with the size and structure of the budget than with the follow-up of EOMs (Interview #51).

In the previous financial framework 2006–2013, slightly less than one-quarter of the EIDHR budget was spent on EOMs (cf. European Commission, 2011a). The debate in COHOM centred on whether this share should be maintained (or even formalized), whether it should be abandoned and the EOMs financed from geographical instruments, or whether even a bigger share of the EIDHR budget should be directly connected to the EOMs and their follow-up. The debate was complicated by the fact that there were different views not only among the member states, but also between DG DEVCO and the EEAS. While DG DEVCO is responsible for disbursement of the general EIDHR money, the budget for EOMs is managed by the Service for Foreign Policy Instruments within the EEAS. It was, as a result, part of the ongoing delimitation of power between the Commission and the EEAS (Interview #51). In the end, the COHOM took the middle ground and supported the earmarking of up to 25 per cent of the EIDHR budget for EOMs, as had been the case in the past. Although the attribution did not find its way into the text of the regulation proper, it was codified in a joint declaration of the Parliament, Council, and Commission that was attached to the regulation and published in the Official Journal (European Parliament and Council, 2014b).[2]

On the issue of the EOMs' follow-up, the debate was not as polarized as on the budget. The main issue on the table was the relationship between the EOMs' recommendations, the rest of the EIDHR-funded projects and the programming of other instruments of external action. In this case, the call of some member states for a more prominent role of the EOMs' recommendations in shaping subsequent EU funding in the target country stumbled over the Commission's (and the Parliament's) reluctance to subordinate long-term planning of development assistance to political considerations. In the end, the language on the implementation of the EOMs' recommendations was significantly strengthened in the new EIDHR regulation, but the Commission's autonomy in programming other instruments was maintained. The regulation explicitly stated that the EU is interested in 'all stages of the electoral cycle' and aims to fund 'measures aimed at the consistent integration of electoral processes into the democratic cycle, disseminating information on and implementing recommendations made by EU EOMs' (European Parliament and Council, 2014b: Art. 2.1.d). In addition, the list of EIDHR objectives, which constitutes an annex to the regulation, states in relation to the EOMs that 'the approach encompassing all stages of the electoral cycle, including follow-up activities, will be further developed with complementary actions between bilateral programming and EIDHR projects' (European Parliament and Council, 2014b: Annex).

At the same time, the negotiations showed that there was an agreement that the various tools that the EU could use, such as political dialogue, HoMs' reports, and technical assistance, should be better coordinated to support implementation of its election observation missions (Interview #50; Interview #52). Since 2015, the Commission has been funding a new NGO-run project that aims at increasing the coherence between democracy promotion and development assistance by mainstreaming civil society considerations into all other policies (Interview #54). In general, the role of local actors in supporting democratic elections across the whole election cycle has been strengthened in the EU's approach, even though it may take time to show in the actual practice. The emphasis on local actors has been deliberate. The EU is ready to support the implementation of the EOMs' recommendations, but does not want to be responsible for this, because that would enable the local actors to shift the blame to the EU in case of insufficient progress (Interview #50).

The European Parliament did not play a major role in the negotiations because it was happy with the result of the Council negotiations. In principle, both the EU funding of democracy and human rights and, particularly, the organization of EU EOMs, in which the MEPs play an important role, enjoy broad support across the parliamentary groups (Interview #40).

Czech interest and engagement in EU Election Observation Missions

A focus on democracy and human rights has been an important constituent of Czech foreign policy since 1989. Under the influence of former dissidents, in particular Václav Havel, the president between 1989 and 2003 and his associates who served in various senior positions in Czech diplomacy and politics, Czech foreign policy identified human rights and democracy as 'principles' of foreign policy in Czech conceptual documents (Government of the Czech Republic, 1999, 2003). The emphasis went beyond mere declaration, however, and in 2005, a special Department for Human Rights and Transition Promotion was established at the Foreign Ministry (cf. Bartovic, 2008). Over the years, the Czech Republic supported transition to democracy, civil rights defenders, and election processes, among others, across the world, focused on but not limited to target countries where the Czechs' own experience with transformation could offer useful lessons, such as Belarus, Ukraine, and Cuba (Ministry of Foreign Affairs, 2010). The consensus on the prioritization of human rights and democracy in foreign policy may be slowly giving way in Czech politics (cf. Weiss, 2015a), but support for human rights and democracy using foreign policy instruments nominally still remains among key foreign policy objectives (Government of the Czech Republic, 2015a).

As a result, Czech representatives have traditionally been active in emphasizing the promotion of democracy and human rights at the EU level and internationally. At the COHOM level, the Czech Republic has been considered an actor that actively follows the agenda and speaks on the selected points of interest (Interview #42). Beyond the working group activity, for example, the Czech Republic actively supported the creation of the Eastern Partnership Civil Society Forum and convened its first meeting during the Czech EU Council presidency in 2009. It has also regularly contributed to election observation missions both under the framework of the EU and the ODIHR/OSCE, although it may not have been particularly successful in the mission participants selection procedure in the EU (Interview #43). In addition, the Foreign Ministry's transition promotion budget has financed a number of projects touching upon free and fair elections within the international context, both more generally, such as supporting media freedom and freedom of speech in the target countries, and more specifically, such as a 2011 project supporting implementation of the EU EOMs' recommendations in Sierra Leone (Gabriel et al., 2011; Ministry of Foreign Affairs of the Czech Republic, 2013). Every year since 2013, the Czech Republic has also presented a resolution on equal participation at the UN Human Rights Council (Ministry of Foreign Affairs of the Czech Republic, 2015a).

At the EU level, the Czech Republic has followed the issue of democratic elections and EOMs for a long time. There are several reasons behind the Czech interest in this topic. First, it falls within the general focus on democratic transition, in which democratic elections play a crucial role. Second, due to the limited staffing of the human rights and transformation policy department at the ministry, the officer representing the country in the capital-based COHOM serves as the national focal point for election observation missions at the same time. As a result, the concentration on election observation within the broader COHOM agenda is a logical consequence of the knowledge at hand of the individual representative (Interview #49; Interview #51).

Formulation of the Czech negotiation position

It has already been asserted that the drafting of the new EIDHR directive was a planned exercise within the context of preparation of the new multi-annual financial framework. It was no surprise for any of the involved actors and the Czech Republic was no exception. The formulation of the Czech negotiation position needs to be understood within the broader context of its long-term engagement in and approach to the EIDHR in general and the election observation missions in particular.

The policy of human rights and democracy support is institutionally firmly stationed at the Foreign Ministry. As there is no significant overlap with the work of other ministries, the policy is one of the examples of an agenda that does not usually pass through all the formal approval procedures through the ministry's Sectorial Coordination Group, but instead the position springs up from within the human rights and transition policy department in consultation with other relevant desks and the permanent representation in Brussels. This is also the case of the election observation agenda, which had been shaped by the department and the PSC section at the permanent representation.

In line with its long-term policy, the Czech Republic formulated several general priorities for the EIDHR regulation negotiation and one specific one. Overall, the Czechs supported the further existence of a separate EIDHR and wanted to strengthen its democracy-related activities, which had been sidelined by the human rights agenda. As the EOMs constituted one of the core activities of the EU in support of democracy, the Czechs were in favour of maintaining the set share of the EIDHR budget earmarked for election observation. Specifically, the Czech Republic wanted the EU to pay more attention to the follow-up of EOMs. This should be reflected both in the text of the EIDHR regulation and in the composition of the budget. In the text, the follow-up should gain a more prominent position in the EIDHR scope and objectives. In the budget, not only should 25 per cent of the total budget be set aside for the observation missions, but on top of that extra money from the remaining 75 per cent should be assigned for the implementation of the missions' recommendations (Interview #49).

The choice of the specific priorities for the EIDHR negotiations not only fit into the general Czech objectives and preferences, but it was also based on pragmatic reasons. Election observation is a generally accepted activity with established actors that have mastered significant expertise both at the EU level and internationally. Very few, however, have focused on the follow-up of the observation missions and especially on the fate of the missions' recommendations. The decision by Czech diplomacy to raise the topic at the EU level was driven by a sense of effectiveness (the EU should be interested in what comes out of the observation missions when spending money on them) as well as the perceived opportunity to fill a niche and raise the profile of the Czech Republic as an engaged actor. In the words of one of the diplomats, the topic 'was just lying there and was free to seize' both in the EU and at the UN level (Interview #40).

Czech activity during the negotiations

The EIDHR negotiation was just one in a series of various meetings that touched upon election observation in the EU. The Czech interest in the follow-up of observation missions had preceded this particular round of negotiations and could be observed both in Brussels and in bilateral activities. The issue became part of all instructions related to election observation. For example, the PSC ambassador was raising the question of missions' follow-up constantly during the regular PSC meetings on where the EU should deploy the EOMs in future (Interview #53). It also appeared in the speaking points of deputy ministers travelling to Brussels (Interview #40) as well as in the foreign minister's speaking points on the EU human rights agenda (Interview #49). When the Czech representative raised the point again at the COHOM level during the EIHDR negotiations, it was a standard intervention that could be expected by the partners. And even though the PSC did not have to debate the EIDHR regulation in the end, the Czechs were prepared to raise the issue at the higher level again if necessary (Interview #53).

In addition, the Czech representatives had asked for the possibility to use EU money to support implementation of the EU EOMs' recommendations in the past. In 2012, the Czech Republic proposed such a project in Sierra Leone, having funded its own small project there a year before, but the local EU delegation refused to finance such an endeavour from the EIDHR money due to the fact that this type of project was not included in the annual action programme. Ever since, the Czechs had emphasized the need for a change in informal meetings with Commission and EEAS officials (Interview #40).

Since the issue of the missions' follow-up was not on the EU agenda for the first time, there was a group of countries that were traditionally interested in changing the current practice. The Czech negotiators could count on their support and also got it. In addition, as there was a general agreement in the institutions that the follow-up constituted a weak point of the EU's engagement in electoral processes in transition countries, the stronger language that the Czechs requested had already been included in the draft and was further reinforced during the negotiations. The Czech Republic was one of the countries that was consulted bilaterally by the COHOM chair specifically on the election language in the regulation (Interview #49).

The assertion that the EU needed to do more in terms of the missions' follow-up was strengthened by the Czech idea to earmark additional money for this purpose. The proposal met with strong opposition from the Commission that considered it an encroachment on its prerogatives, particularly its autonomy in disbursement of the EU budget. At the same time, the request for more money for EOMs and their follow-up could have an impact on the debate about whether there should be specific money for the EOMs at all, which was discussed by the COHOM. The result, which codified the existing practice, but did not bite off the remaining three-quarters of the budget, was, in the end, acceptable both for the Czechs and for the institutions.

The Czech activity was centred on the negotiations in the Council. Although the European Parliament was an important player in the actual adoption of the regulation, the Czech representatives did not feel the need to engage with the Parliament in any manner. The Parliament was in favour of both the continuation of EOMs, in which it plays an important part, and the stronger language on the missions' follow-up in line with the Czech preference. In addition, the Parliament does not take part in the adoption of EIDHR programming documents, namely the multi-annual and annual programmes, and is therefore not seen as an important actor on the issue of EOMs (Interview #40).

The EIDHR programmes have been crucial in changing the practice of the EOMs. The EIDHR regulation is simply an enabler for the EU to pay more attention to missions' follow-up. Therefore, the Czech activity did not stop in 2013 with the compromise on the regulation, but continued during the subsequent preparation of the programming documents and the debates on changes in the methodology of EU EOMs. Again, the Czech position was asserted both at the level of COHOM and the PSC level and the Czechs were closely consulted on the methodology for election observation missions that was drafted and negotiated in summer 2015.

Evaluation of the Czech engagement

From the perspective of the lobbying literature, the Czech performance in the EIDHR negotiations and effort to increase the EU activity in the follow-up of election observation missions seems to be close to the ideal. The Czech representatives were able to combine long-term engagement with clearly defined objectives that were supported by bilateral commitments as well as activity at the international level. Their position and preferences had been known long before the actual negotiations started and had already been reflected in the original proposal, and during the negotiations they were also considered instrumental in safeguarding the designated part of the EIDHR budget for EOMs (Interview #52). What contributed to this success story?

First, the support for human rights and democracy is a policy shaped by a very limited and stable set of actors in the Czech Republic. It is concentrated around the single Department of Human Rights and Transition Promotion at the Foreign Ministry, which manages the bilateral funding programmes, the Czech human rights-related activity in the UN, as well as negotiations at the EU level where it prepares the instructions and sends out the Czech representatives to COHOM. This has not changed with the establishment of the Brussels-based COHOM, which is attended by a diplomat that previously worked for the department in Prague (this person has also taken over the Czech participation in the EIDHR committee). The Czech representative to the capital-based COHOM has served there for ten years, and as a result he has been able to establish a wide network of contacts in the institutions, other member states, and relevant NGOs. Being, as was already mentioned, the Czech focal point for election observation at the same time, he also has a wide network of contacts and extensive expertise on the EU EOMs. In the studied case, as a result, Czech diplomacy could rely on a combination of knowledge of the process as well as the substance.

Second, there was good communication between various levels of Czech activity. At the lower level this was made easier by the concentration of all types of engagement, uni/bilateral, European and international, within the single department at the Foreign Ministry. But the lower level activity gained strong backing at the level of the management, particularly at the level of the PSC, but also at higher levels, including the minister. This amplified the message sent by the Czechs on the EIDHR reform.

Third, the objectives were well defined and relevant for the EU as a whole. By concentrating on the EOMs' follow-up, the Czechs could rely on expert backing, because the insufficiency of the EU's performance in this respect had been criticized in the past. It also appealed to those that were not particularly interested in the topic, but wanted to raise the effectiveness of the EU's external action. After all, the EU had been spending large sums on organization of the EOMs and the EU seemed to be wasting money by not following up on their recommendations.

Fourth, the Czech activity was not limited to a single negotiation, but was part of a longer-term effort to improve the EU policy on EOMs. The Czechs acquired a reputation of being interested in the topic and became insiders that were consulted in advance. Above all, the fact that the Czechs invested from the national budget in a pilot project that should support implementation of the EOMs' recommendations raised the Czech profile and persuaded the institutions that the Czechs took it seriously (Interview #43). The Foreign Ministry's budget line on transformation promotion also ensures that there are a number of Czech NGOs that are active in democracy and human rights support that could run the pilot and would be able to make use of the EU money for the EOMs' follow-up when available.[3]

To sum up, the Czech Republic was able to acquire insider status on the topic of EU election observation missions and their follow-up, which contributed to the successful performance during the 2013 negotiations on the new EIDHR regulation. In fact, there was very limited effort invested during the actual negotiations, because the key points had already been included in the original draft by the European Commission. This was partly a result of the changing understanding of the situation among the EU institutions that followed from the lessons learned during the EU's performance, but also, at least partly, a product of continuous Czech pressure for a change. A clear objective in combination with expertise and a well-developed network of contacts of the key negotiator constituted the basis of this example of successful interest promotion in EU foreign policy.

Notes

1 Where there is an agreement among all three institutions on the final text of a proposed document, the original proposal is amended by the Parliament in line with the agreement in the first reading and the other two institutions give their consent to the amendments. This procedure allows the proposal to be adopted in the first reading and in the shortest time possible. For an external observer it may be a bit misleading,

however, because it hints at a stronger role of the Parliament in the process than is actually true.
2 It should be noted that the total budget of the EIDHR shrank during the negotiations by €250 million compared to the original Commission proposal. This was not, however, the result of the COHOM activity, but the result of the general debate on the size of the EU's budget for the period 2014–2020 and particularly of the net payers' demands.
3 Even though it actually was a Slovak NGO that ran the pilot in Sierra Leone in this particular case.

7 Common Security and Defence Policy

Extending the mandate for EUMM Georgia in 2014

The Common Security and Defence Policy is very specific compared to other EU external relations tools. The difference does not necessarily stem from the decision-making procedure, because unanimity is generally the rule in all of the Common Foreign and Security Policy as well as on other issues. Rather, the CSDP is the policy area where the EU is most dependent on its member states, their capabilities, and their willingness to commit themselves beyond the general consensus in the Council. Due to the fact that the EU does not possess any military or civilian capabilities, the personnel under the EU flag can be deployed only when member states pledge sufficient forces (for which they must pay) and sufficient financial resources to cover common costs (for military operations, not for the civilian missions where the common costs are covered from the EU budget) on top of reaching political agreement on the mission. This showed most painfully in the case of the EU military operations in Chad and the Central African Republic, where five force generating conferences were necessary to gather enough capabilities to launch the mission in 2008 (Helly, 2009).

The dependence on member states' capabilities means that besides other factors that determine a country's power and influence on the policy, the existence and size of capabilities and the willingness to deploy them plays a significant role in CSDP. This helps explain the French and British predominance in the policy, the Nordic authority on civilian crisis management, and the perceived rise of Czech influence after the country's decision to contribute to the EU operation in Mali (Interview #10; cf. Fiott, 2015; Korski and Gowan, 2009; Duke, 2009; Jakobsen, 2009). It also increases the role of the relevant Council bodies representing member states, in particular the Political and Security Committee (PSC) and the Committee for Civilian Aspects of Crisis Management (CivCom), that participate in policy implementation to such an extent that they are often accused of micromanagement (Interview #38; Korski and Gowan, 2009).

After its establishment, the European External Action Service incorporated the crisis management bodies that were originally part of the Council secretariat and also took over the chairmanship and agenda-setting in the relevant Council committees and working groups from the rotating presidency.

This does not mean, however, that the Commission is not relevant for the policy. In fact, the respective Commission's services play an ever growing role as the EU strives for a comprehensive approach to crisis management, in which the actual CSDP mission is but a part of a coordinated long-term effort (European Commission and High Representative of the Union for Foreign Affairs and Security Policy, 2013; European Council, 2013; Gross, 2008). Coordination between the various EU policies has been lacking for a long time though and one of the Lisbon Treaty's objectives when establishing the double-hatted High Representative and the EEAS was exactly to find a remedy (cf. Gauttier, 2004; Koenig, 2011; Reynaert, 2012; Stewart, 2008).

The civilian crisis management missions have often been labelled as the most important added value of the CSDP (Dwan, 2005: 277; Jakobsen, 2006: 299). So far, about two-thirds of the more than 30 missions that the EU has deployed in the world have been civilian. The missions are planned and run by the EEAS's Civilian Planning and Conduct Capability (CPCC) under the political guidance of the CivCom and the PSC and the mandate is approved by the Council (see Korski and Gowan, 2009: 77 for the overview of the planning process). The Council decision always specifies the length of the mission's mandate and, if necessary, approves an extension or any change in its focus, size, and priorities. There is an extensive strategic review preceding every change to the mission's mandate that is prepared by the Crisis Management and Planning Directorate (CMPD) of the EEAS (cf. Gebhard, 2009), the mission itself, as well as the EU delegation and the heads of member states' embassies (HoMs) on the ground. The PSC debates the review in general terms first, then the CivCom discusses it in detail and issues recommendations. On this basis, the CPCC prepares the new concept of operations and operational plan for the member states' approval. The strategic review is thus an important point that determines the shape and focus of the mission in the following period, because the actual Council decision usually occurs very shortly before the old mandate expires and there is political pressure not to leave the mission without a mandate (cf. Lidington, 2014).

Motivation and proposal for change

The European Union Monitoring Mission in Georgia (EUMM) was launched in October 2008 following the Russian–Georgian war the preceding summer. Its role is to monitor the administrative borderlines between Georgia proper and the separatist territories of Abkhazia and South Ossetia and to contribute to a long-term solution to the conflicts. Originally, the mission comprised 200 European monitors that were deployed in Tbilisi and three regional offices. There were four main tasks set for the mission: stabilization, normalization, confidence building, and information (Council of the European Union, 2008). In short, the mission should monitor and analyse the processes on the ground in terms of force movements, the rule of law situation, and institution building, and provide first-hand information to the EU institutions and the member states on the situation on the ground.

The EU played a decisive role in concluding the ceasefire agreement during the hot phase of the conflict and was able to launch the EUMM extremely quickly (Freire and Simão, 2013: 471). The mission, together with a newly established EU special representative (EUSR) for the crisis in Georgia, strengthened the already extensive EU presence in the country, which included the European Commission delegation, the EUSR for the Southern Caucasus, and 15 member states' embassies (Fischer, 2009: 388). Although the EU presence, which had mostly been technical, had not prevented the war, the EU paradoxically increased its influence in 2008 (Bardakçı, 2010: 216), even more so after the withdrawal of the OSCE and UN missions in 2008 and 2009 respectively following a Russian veto, which left the EU as the only international actor with monitors on the ground.

The EU's engagement, including the EUMM, was, however, unable to reach long-term stabilization and contribute to conflict resolution in Georgia (cf. Weiss et al., 2013). The EUMM concluded memoranda of understanding with the Georgian ministries of interior and defence and succeeded in putting in place some confidence-building measures, such as the Incident Prevention and Reporting Mechanism to exchange information between the Georgian authorities and the de facto authorities of the breakaway regions. Its monitoring functions were, however, severely limited since the mission is not allowed to enter the territories of Abkhazia and South Ossetia and must rely on substitute tools, such as satellite imaging (Freire and Simão, 2013). As a result, some EU member states started questioning the effectiveness of the EUMM and the rationality of maintaining the mission in place in its current form in the run-up to the 2014 strategic review.

Negotiation framework and results

The debate on the 2014 EUMM revision started 'extremely early' (Interview #38) in comparison to other missions' strategic reviews. It was launched by an informal report by the CMPD on the previous achievements of the EUMM and possible future developments in summer 2013, even before the EUMM's new mandate was adopted by the Council in September 2013 (Council of the European Union, 2013). In the informal negotiations that followed, two groups of member states crystallized (Interview #31). The first group, where many of the bigger member states were present, pushed for winding the mission down due to the limited results that had been achieved and the limited room for manoeuvre caused by political constraints that suggested that there was not much chance of more success in future. The second group of countries, which was larger but consisted mainly of smaller member states, wanted to maintain the EUMM in its present size.

The two groups did not disagree as much in their evaluation of the situation on the ground and the potential of the EUMM to make a difference as in the political importance of the mission. The latter group understood a potential reduction as a wrong political gesture towards Georgia, Russia, and the two separatist entities. For the advocates of reduction, efficiency was the main objective and they argued that as the mission was unlikely to achieve any breakthrough, there was no point in spending money (on average over €20 million per year from the CFSP budget plus additional money from the member states' pockets) on so many monitors and tasks (Interview #30; cf. Council of the European Union, 2013).

The positions of member states' representatives in CivCom on the future of the EUMM were 'very polarized' (Interview #31). The advocates of prolongation therefore sought to change the negotiation dynamics, connect the stalled debate to the general development of the CSDP and find a new *raison d'être* for the mission (Interview #30; Interview #38). This materialized in a joint non-paper coordinated by the Netherlands that suggested strengthening of the confidence-building part of the EUMM's tasks, which would make the EUMM a good example of the new EU approach emphasizing the comprehensive approach endorsed by the December European Council (European Council, 2013). A joint meeting of CivCom and COEST, with the participation of EEAS and Commission representatives, was organized to discuss what measures could be included and how. The objective was to expand the usually narrow focus of the strategic review to better embrace the broader context of the mission (Interview #38).

In the end, it was exactly the context that changed the whole negotiation dynamic. The crisis in Ukraine and, in particular, the Russian annexation of Crimea persuaded the sceptics that it was crucial to maintain the EUMM in its present size despite the doubts about its efficiency (Interview #25; Interview #30; Interview #38; cf. Foreign and Commonwealth Office, 2014). The strategic review was issued in April 2014 by the CMPD without major controversies (EEAS, 2014) and the Council adopted the new mandate in December 2014 (Council of the European Union, 2014). In fact, the Council consolidated the mission in its existing form by extending the mandate by two years for the first time since 2008, even though the mission's yearly budget decreased slightly to €18 million. The number of monitors remained unchanged and the mission's contribution to the comprehensive approach was strengthened by the establishment of a "Project Cell" to reach out to other member states' and third states' activities in Georgia related to the EUMM's objectives.

Czech interest and engagement in the CSDP

For a long time, the Czech Republic tended to be rather sceptical about the CSDP. Unlike NATO, the European Union was not considered a reliable security guarantor and the development of autonomous European capabilities was seen as undermining the transatlantic link and threatening the US commitment to European defence. This scepticism never did go as far as making the Czech Republic resign from CSDP altogether and seek a Danish-style opt-out, but the priority of the Czech foreign and security policy lay clearly with NATO (see above in Chapter 2). The EU's role was seen mainly in the framework of 'the development of EU crisis management capabilities' (Government of the Czech Republic, 2011b: 11).

Step by step, this perception changed. Following the disagreement with the Obama administration about the abandoned plan for a third site of the ballistic missile defence system in Central Europe, the Czech politicians started paying more attention to the EU. Most importantly, the Czech Republic decided to contribute militarily to the CSDP operation EUTM Mali, which was deployed well outside any Czech region of traditional interest. In formal strategic documents, however, the shift has been reflected just very slightly: The newest security strategy of 2015 preserves most of the formulations of the preceding document and only develops the necessity of effective EU–NATO cooperation more (Government of the Czech Republic, 2015c).

The Czech warming-up to the civilian crisis management of the CSDP had come a bit earlier. The 2009 European Council on Foreign Relations' report on EU civilian capabilities still counted the Czech Republic among the 'agnostics' (Korski and Gowan, 2009), but civilian crisis management was already one of the topics on the agenda of the Czech EU Council presidency in the same year. Since then, the civilian missions have belonged to Czech priorities (Interview #25). The Czech Republic has contributed to a number of them, in particular the EULEX Kosovo, which was deployed in this region of utmost interest for the Czech Republic, but also in other places, including the EUMM Georgia.

Several parts of the state administration are responsible for managing the Czech contribution to the EU's CSDP. Whereas the government and the parliament are the ultimate strategic decision-makers in terms of whether the Czech Republic contributes to a particular mission and under which mandates, the line ministries manage the day-to-day business. Quite logically, there is an important role for the Defence Ministry when planning and conducting participation in military missions and of the Interior Ministry when it comes to police missions. In general, however, the Czech contribution is coordinated by the Foreign Ministry. The National Focal Point at the Foreign Ministry maintains a database of Czech experts available for civilian missions and organizes regular preparatory courses for interested persons. Nevertheless, a need arises occasionally to consult the preparation of civilian missions beyond the traditional institutional actors, the MFA, and the Interior Ministry. The character of some missions requires specific skills and knowledge that are not available in the general population and cannot be trained in the short term. The EUMM is a case in point, because the monitoring of force movements and build-up requires military expertise. Many of the Czech participants were, therefore, soldiers who were temporarily released from the service in order to be able to take part in the civilian mission. A close cooperation with the Defence Ministry was therefore necessary in this particular case.

Similarly, the Foreign Ministry personnel manage the Czech participation in Council decision-making bodies, particularly the PSC and CivCom (whereas a soldier represents the country in the EU Military Committee). In comparison to the military branch of the CSDP, where senior military officers take part in the Council negotiations as a rule, junior diplomats are often members of the CivCom (cf. Davis Cross, 2010: 12). The Czech Republic is no exception in this case and the country has been sending junior diplomats to this committee. Yet this limits the country's influence, because the few countries that do send a senior diplomat to CivCom are able to shape the policy better (Interview #31).

Formulation of the Czech negotiation position

The Czech Republic was, from the beginning, a staunch supporter of the EUMM Georgia. Eastern Europe had belonged to the declared priorities of Czech foreign policy (see Chapter 5; cf. Weiss, 2011) and there was a limited role that any other organization could play at the moment. Czechs had participated in the mission right from its start and sustained, at the time of writing, the fourth biggest national contingent of 16 personnel (EEAS, 2015b).

The Czech position was formulated in consultations with other member states as well as with the Czech EUMM personnel who provided first-hand experience from the ground (Interview #38). The expertise from within the mission was important, although Czechs had not been able to advance to management positions in the EUMM and thus their strategic understanding of the situation may have been limited.[1] Unlike with the personnel in the mission, there was not any consultation with Czechs within the EEAS. Although there had been Czech presence in the EU civilian crisis management bodies for many years, there was never a systematic effort to use this contact for better access to information or to gain better understanding of the institutions' motivations and thinking (Interview #20).

After the first round of consultations (with Germany and with Czech EUMM personnel), the Foreign Ministry was rather sceptical about the future of the mission. Obstacles seemed to prevail for the mission to continue in its current form and with its current objectives. Therefore, the ministry inclined to join those member states that called for winding the mission down. This changed, however, when an active group of member states started pushing for maintaining the EUMM in its existing size. This group consisted of traditional Czech allies on East European policy issues, notably Sweden, Poland, and the Baltic states, and in the end the Czech Republic decided to support them (Interview #38). Once the decision to preserve the mission was made, there remained the question of the specific mandate, which was supposed to create a more stable environment and realistic expectations for the EUMM.

As a result, Czech diplomacy entered the latter stages of negotiations on the EUMM strategic review and Council decision with three priorities. First, the mission should be preserved in its existing size, i.e. with 200 monitors along the administrative borderlines with Abkhazia and South Ossetia. Second, unlike in all previous decisions, the Council should approve the mission mandate for two years, which would allow for longer-term planning and send a signal to Georgian, Russian, and the separatist regions' authorities that the EU remained interested in solving the frozen conflicts in Georgia. Finally, the mission should focus on confidence-building measures (CBMs) as the new cornerstone of the EU's activity.

Czech activity during the negotiations

As mentioned above, the Czech Republic entered the negotiations without a clear-cut preference and its position crystallized only during the first phase of the debate. It thus was joining an already existing cooperation and cannot be regarded as an originator or organizer of a like-minded group. It did, however, contribute actively to the group's efforts during the later phases of negotiations. It also supported a Swedish–Polish non-paper that argued for the mission's preservation (Interview #30).

There was a need to find a new rationale for the mission to justify its continuation despite the objective problems on the ground. Besides the motion to uphold the EUMM led by Sweden with active contribution by the Poles and the Baltic states, the Czechs also actively supported the initiative to strengthen the EU's activities in confidence-building measures led by the Dutch and Italians, which was part of the broader CSDP debate leading to the December European Council on defence. The Czech permanent representation proposed to connect the two debates and frame the prolongation of the EUMM as an example of a CSDP mission that already reflected the new priorities. As a result, a joint meeting of CivCom and COEST was organized with Commission's input that discussed the CBMs and their application in the Georgian situation (Interview #38).

The Czech activity concentrated on the Council debate. This seemed logical given the fact that the CSDP is largely intergovernmental policy that relies on unanimous agreement of the member states. Moreover, due to the polarization of the debate, the EEAS, although preparing the draft strategic review and chairing the CivCom (and PSC), was not in a position to push anything through very quickly. Rather, it waited for a common position to crystallize from the Council debates. The refocusing on the issue of CBMs was meant to provide the Council with a solid point around which the agreement could be built.

The Visegrád Group that usually works together on East European topics failed to provide a working platform in the case of the EUMM. Hungary and Slovakia kept a low profile in the debate, as they did not seem to be interested in the fate of the mission. Poland, on the other hand, was a very active participant and one of the agenda drivers. Czech–Polish consultations occurred regularly, but Poland had other informal fora in which to discuss the issue, most importantly bilateral cooperation with Sweden, which was based not only on shared views but also on good relations between the foreign ministers, and the Weimar group (Interview #30; Interview #38).

To a large extent, the crisis in Ukraine made the whole debate and various initiatives obsolete. Yet, the new Council decision largely reflected the Czech priorities: it did maintain the number of monitors at 200 and it did, for the first time, contain a mandate for two years, instead of 12–15 months. The confidence-building measures were not highlighted specifically in the decision, though. They just remained one of the mission's objectives. It can be argued, however, that the CBMs were meant as an alternative focus point in a situation when some member states were not ready to support the mission in its existing form, rather than a priority in itself. Leaving the CBMs out did not therefore harm the Czech interests very much. And, after all, the CBM part of the mandate was to some extent upgraded by strengthening the EUMM's cooperation with other actors in Georgia through the establishment of the Project Cell as part of the effort to approach the situation more comprehensively.

Evaluation of the Czech engagement

Reviewing a mandate for an ongoing CSDP mission is a continuous process, not a one-off negotiation. Especially in the case of the EUMM Georgia, the mission had been deployed for five years when the negotiations on the newest strategic review and new mandate started in 2013. That means that the member states cannot have been surprised to see the dossier on the agenda; they know that a new mandate for the mission would have to be prepared each time the old one is about to expire. Having said that, the situation on the ground might change quite rapidly either as a result of the mission's activity or as a result of a changing context. Similarly, the European institutions' and other Council members' views of the mission develop continuously and the member states need to be aware of this when entering the negotiations.

For this type of ongoing agenda, the key stakeholders establish themselves in time. In CivCom business, the Czech Republic suffers from a 'bad image' in general that usually implies 'smaller perceived weight' during the negotiations (Interview #31). When the EEAS and CivCom chair invites the smaller group of countries for consultations, the Czech Republic is not, as a rule, among them. There are several examples of missions, however, where the Czech Republic has been recognized as an actor and the EUMM Georgia is one of them (together with EULEX Kosovo and EUBAM Rafah) (Interview #31). In this concrete case of the 2014 EUMM Georgia decision, the Czech Republic was indeed seen as an active negotiator by other member states' representatives (Interview #30).

Czech diplomacy was active from the first phases of decision-making, although there remained some room for improvement. Active consultations with other member states and with Czech nationals in the mission provided timely information about other member states' positions as well as about the situation on the ground. Access to first-hand information from the region and the mission is crucial for a member state's influence during the Council negotiation because the EEAS, which steers the process, feeds the CivCom and the PSC with processed information only and its reports naturally emphasize facts that support the Service's proposals (Interview #29). The Czech Republic had a weaker link to the Service itself and given the junior positions that the Czech nationals occupied in the EUMM, their information could be patchy, lacking a broader perspective, and the Czech Foreign Ministry did not have first-hand access to the mission leadership's report to the EEAS.

A relatively wide spectrum of methods was employed in preparation for and during the negotiations. Consultations with other member states were commonplace, including focusing on the big (or bigger) states Germany and Poland. The Czechs actively engaged in coalition-building and even tried to modify and expand the coalition by shifting the emphasis to attract broader support. This effort consisted of apt reframing of the EUMM debate to fit within the broader and more important discussion of the moment, namely the preparation of the European Council on defence, and to accentuate the confidence-building measures in the mission's mandate at the expense of mere monitoring. This would make the EUMM not only an attempt to contribute to conflict resolution in Georgia, which was important for some but less vital for others, but also sort of a pilot project in a comprehensive approach, which was important for the EU as a whole. It also had the potential to change the dynamics of the negotiations by expanding the number of players by including the COEST delegates and, most importantly, the Commission, which had been present all the time, but gained an elevated role once the issue transformed from a monitoring mission only into a comprehensive approach type of activity.

The Czech activity concentrated on the Council and, to a large extent, this seems a reasonable decision, because other institutions have a very limited say in this particular type of EU activity. The Commission's role is obviously important, because they 'sit on the money' (Interview #31). But the political agreement in the Council is more important. Once the member states decide to uphold the mission and commit their personnel and resources, it would be very difficult for the Commission to withdraw their part of the funding. Similarly, the institutional landscape was very simple on the domestic front where the Foreign Ministry did not need to specifically consult any changes to the EUMM mandate with other ministries or offices beyond the standard approval procedure for any EU-related instruction. There was no specific consultation outside the civil service either. The negotiation and decision-making seemed to be very Brussels-centred with occasional outreach to the foreign ministries and their direct consultations (such as the initial Czech–German consultations that occurred directly between Prague and Berlin).

To sum up, the preparation of the 2014 EUMM Council decision revealed the role of the Czech Republic as perhaps a secondary actor, but still an actor. An actor that does not set the agenda, table proposals, and participate in all relevant meetings, but an actor that has a clearly defined position, cooperates with other actors within the issue alliance, and is able to contribute to the debate with original ideas. Yet, it also showed how elusive and problematic the efforts to promote one's interests can be in EU foreign policy, in particular in the CSDP. The polarization in the Council that emerged from the initial round of negotiations and that all subsequent proposals tried to overcome disappeared overnight due to the change of the external context, in this case Russia's annexation of Crimea.

Note

1 This is a structural deficiency in Czech CSDP participation and has been recognized as such by the Foreign Ministry (Interview #25). Despite relatively active participation in civilian missions, the Czechs have rarely reached positions in the missions' management with the notable exception of the Chief Prosecutor in EULEX Kosovo between 2012 and 2014.

8 Conclusions

This book has asked how the Czech Republic, as a small and new member state of the European Union, pursues its interest in EU foreign policy-making. While a lot of academic attention has been paid to the content of member states' policies and the resulting EU positions as well as the success rate of individual member states' efforts to upload their policy preferences into EU policies, relatively little is known about the methods that member states use to make their points in EU negotiations. By offering a study of the Czech Republic's interest promotion in EU foreign policy, this book has tried to help fill this gap in the literature and offer new insights into EU decision-making. It has done so by grounding the analysis in two sets of literature: on Europeanization and on lobbying. The key point of departure has been the idea that the member states adjust their behaviour in the Council in the long term as they learn the environment and better understand the dynamics of EU decision-making, but they promote their positions rationally in individual cases. In addition, it has been assumed that in their behaviour small member states in the Council resemble advocates for private interest and, as a result, findings from the lobbying literature can be applied to the study of their behaviour in the EU. Three working hypotheses were formulated on the basis of these two sets of literature.

The research was based on a combination of a small-scale survey and a comparative case study method. A small-N survey of Czech representatives in selected Council working groups and committees between 2004 and 2015 served to confront the theoretical expectations with the perceptions of the practitioners of their everyday work. Moreover, the survey offered a number of additional insights into the patterns of their behaviour and their career development. Altogether, the survey sought the answer to the question of how the Czech Republic promotes its positions in EU foreign policy negotiations.

The case studies have provided a detailed look into individual occasions on which the Czech representatives aimed at influencing the final EU policy in four distinct policy areas. By presenting the Czech position formulation and course of action in the broader context of Czech interests and the development of the agenda at the EU level, the studies aimed at answering why the Czech Republic used particular methods of interest promotion. The four policy areas represented by the cases (and also forming the framework for analysis of the survey data) covered foreign trade, European Neighbourhood Policy, policy in support of democracy and human rights, and Common Security and Defence Policy. They vary in the decision-making procedure, involvement of the EU institutions, as well as in their fit with Czech foreign policy priorities.

In this chapter, the main findings of the research will be presented. The relevance of the research for the literature on Europeanization, the role of small member states in the EU, and the potential of lobbying scholarship for further research on EU decision-making will be discussed. Moreover, preliminary thoughts will be offered on what the findings in the Czech case may say about other member states that are in any respect comparable. Finally, opportunities for further research will be suggested.

Main findings of the book

The Czech Republic has been an EU member only since 2004. As a result, a very limited number of officials have contributed to the formulation of EU foreign policy on behalf of the Czech Republic. While this restricted population partly limits the relevance of the results, it still offers interesting insights in relation to the working hypotheses.

The *first hypothesis* predicted that the longer the Czech Republic is an EU member, the broader the spectrum of interest promotion methods that would be employed by the Czech representatives in the Council. Here the limited population had the biggest impact, because no relevant data could be gained from officials ending their tenure in Brussels between 2005 and 2008. For those that served at the Czech permanent representation between 2009 and 2015 the hypothesis could be confirmed. Although there are big differences between the responses for individual years, the general trend is indeed in accordance with the expectations, namely the respondents claim to use ever more methods in their everyday work at least sometimes. That would mean that the Czech representatives learn how to play the Brussels game and how to use the various options that are at their disposal. Naturally, there is no guarantee that more methods of interest promotion also mean higher success rates, but they provide the state's representatives with more diverse channels of influence.

The *second hypothesis* expected a shift towards more elaborate methods of interest promotion with increasing membership experience. The lobbying literature suggests that some methods are more efficient than just focusing on the negotiated dossier and trying to persuade the partners through bargaining, argumentation, or similar issue-focused methods (group 1 methods). These have been identified as "early warning methods" that aim at getting access to information about issues on the agenda and planned proposals early enough to be able to prepare good negotiation positions and strategies (group 2 methods). And, the most sophisticated methods (group 3), labelled as "methods for obtaining insider status", should ensure that the member state steps out of the line of similar small states, becomes a recognized stakeholder, and is invited to smaller groups for informal consultations that allow it to influence the draft even before it is published.

There has, indeed, been a shift towards group 2 methods in the Czech negotiation practice. This suggests that there has been some learning on the Czech part that corresponds with the expectations of the lobbying literature. Namely, that the Czech representatives have appreciated the value of timely information for their work. In contrast, there has been no significant increase in the use of group 3 methods. In fact, their frequency even slightly decreased when compared to the year 2004 when the Czech Republic joined the EU. This is contrary to what the lobbying literature expects and two alternative explanations can account for this result. First, the Czech representatives may not have recognized the value of this type of methods yet. If this were the case, it would suggest that more than a decade of EU membership is necessary to fully appreciate the internal working of the EU and to incorporate more elaborate ways of interest promotion. Alternatively, the results can be interpreted as the inability of the Czech system of European policy-making to identify issues where the Czech Republic wants to become an insider and/or to prove the Czech stake in the issues, which requires involvement of several parts of the state administration, rather than just activity on the part of the representative in Brussels and his or her managing department in Prague. In short, the Czech representatives have understood the value of insider status, but knowing that the chance of becoming an insider is so slim, they focus rather on other methods of interest promotion.

The rest of the data collected in this research suggest that the latter explanation is more likely true. Active participation of the Czech Republic in the issue area and expertise were considered the most important factors for the Czech ability to promote its interests in EU foreign policy by the survey respondents, preceded only by timely access to information. Both of these factors constitute the core of the group 3 methods – raising expertise and specialization within the policy area. Moreover, the case study on democracy and human rights policy clearly showed that the Czech Republic is, in fact, able to become an insider on a specific issue within a given policy area and that the insider status certainly helps promote the Czech position. On the other hand, as several of the interviewees in the ENP case study suggested, Czech diplomacy has difficulties using existing expertise and involving it in policy-making, noting specifically the limited engagement of Czech embassies in Eastern Europe and non-governmental organizations active in the region and implementing what was being discussed in Brussels. Arguably, the Czech representatives are aware of the value of the insider status and can even see good results, but they just do not strive for it that often.

The *third working hypothesis* focused on the difference between policy areas within broader EU foreign policy. One part of the hypothesis, namely the link between the involvement of EU institutions and mode of decision-making on one hand and the use of more sophisticated methods of interest promotion has not been confirmed. The more complex institutional environment in foreign trade and ENP seems to have an influence on the type of diplomats that are sent to Brussels to represent the Czech Republic in the Council working groups. They are on average more experienced than diplomats who participate on the Czech's behalf in CFSP and CSDP policy-making. The engagement of the institutions and the regular or frequent use of qualified majority voting has, on the other hand, not provoked a more active and more sophisticated approach to the promotion of Czech positions. The pattern has been the same in all policy areas with group 2 methods being used most often and group 3 methods least often. Foreign trade and CSDP, which should stand on the opposite side of the spectrum, proved to rely on group 1 and group 2 methods the most, whereas group 3 methods were most often used in foreign trade and in policy in support of democracy and human rights.

The other part of the hypothesis that expected a relationship between policy salience and the use of more sophisticated methods could be cautiously declared as confirmed by the data. There is a clear difference between the Czech activities in the two parts of ENP, namely the Eastern and Southern focus. The Czech representatives use more methods from all three groups when shaping the EU's policy towards Eastern Europe and the difference is substantial in group 2 methods. In combination with the finding that the Czech negotiators rely on this type of methods and are rather negligent of the group 3 methods, the difference may be considered to support the expected impact of policy salience.

The research has gone beyond the original working hypotheses and there are other important findings that can be inferred from the survey and the case studies.

First and foremost, individuals seem to play a major role in Czech activities in the Council, but in a different way than the role of individuals is usually conceptualized in the literature. So far, the academic accounts have studied the role of the individual in connection with negotiation success and sought the link between an individual's skills and the country's performance (Meerts, 1997; Tallberg, 2008: 698; cf. Hermann et al., 2001) or the link between an individual's learning and socialization processes and the change of a country's behaviour (cf. Beyers and Trondal, 2004; Checkel, 2005; Juncos and Pomorska, 2006; Lewis, 2005). In the Czech case, the role of the individual is instead connected with the effort that the Czech Republic invests in the negotiation of a particular dossier. The case studies revealed that two of the four cases identified by the stakeholders as those where the Czech Republic invested most effort in recent years within the given policy area highly depended on the commitment of the responsible desk officers and their immediate superiors. In the case of the GSP reform, the Czech Republic would probably not have been engaged at all if it had not been for the desk officer who was interested in the issue and prepared an impact analysis that helped identify the Czech interest in the area. The Czech engagement was not the result of a systemic approach to the policy area, but of an ad hoc individual preference. In addition, the interviews within the case studies from both foreign trade and the ENP indicate that the high level of Czech activity was the consequence of good cooperation between the desk officer in Prague, the desk officer at the permanent representation, and the support they got from their superiors both in Prague and in Brussels. The fact that the interviewees needed to stress this cooperation suggests that, again, this cooperation is not automatic in the Czech system, but exceptional and dependent on individuals.

One way to understand the high impact of individuals in the Czech system is to see it as a direct result of the ill-defined national priorities. The survey respondents hinted that the inability to define national interests that would be shared by the political leadership constituted an important factor damaging the Czech performance in the EU. With weak political leadership and insufficiently defined priorities and interests, there is room for individual initiative at the level of desk officers. Moreover, unclear priorities may easily lead to disagreements between various sections of the state administration as well as between the central office and the permanent representation. This is a deficiency that cannot be remedied by gaining more experience with Brussels policy-making or by adjusting administrative structures, because it is dependent on the quality of the political debate in the country and the interest in foreign policy in general.

Second, state size seems to be important in EU decision-making and not that important at the same time. The controversy about state size and its relevance for EU policy-making is one of the most vocal in the academic literature. While some consider size the key element for the country's influence, others emphasize other factors, such as expertise and tactics. This research suggests that the reality is, quite unsurprisingly, a bit more complicated. On one hand, there is the need to distinguish between the objectives of the actor vis-à-vis the dossier on the table. Where the objective is to block an unwanted proposal, size seems to be a crucial variable and the support of big member states is necessary for a small country to be successful in getting rid of undesirable motions. At the same time, however, the ENP case study clearly showed that big member states can effectively cancel each other out. On the other hand, size seems to play a much smaller role when the objective is to promote a positive agenda. The survey respondents had no doubts that size is not an important factor that would determine the Czech influence in the EU or constitute an obstacle to better performance. When asked about the account of their action within an individual dossier, however, cooperation with big member states often featured prominently, as the case studies show. The alliances with the United Kingdom on GSP reform and on more-for-more, and with Germany on more-for-more were crucial. In contrast, in policy areas where the decision-making relies more on unanimity and the intergovernmental approach, the Czech Republic seemed not to seek cooperation with big member states that actively. On the mission in Georgia, for example, Sweden and Poland (arguably not the most important countries in CSDP) were the main partners.

112 *Conclusions*

Third, Visegrád does not seem to be the first port of call for Czech negotiators in the studied cases. With the partial exception of the ENP where all Visegrád countries were members of the same broad like-minded group, Visegrád did not feature in Czech tactics. Nor did it merit any particular attention in the survey on places where the respondents could add their own views of used methods and important factors. This runs counter to various accounts in academic literature that consider Visegrád cooperation an appealing instrument for its member states in EU policy-making (cf. Törö et al., 2014). It instead lends support to the conception of Visegrád as a specific vehicle that may prove important on some issues, but has a number of limitations and is not suitable for all EU agendas (Dangerfield, 2014).

Relevance for the academic literature

This book has aimed at adding new knowledge to the existing literature on Europeanization and EU decision-making. More specifically, it has focused on the methods that a small EU member state employs to promote its priorities in EU foreign policy. In doing so, it has applied insights provided by the lobbying literature. The links of some of the findings to the specific literature has already been presented above. In this section, the more general lessons will be discussed.

First, the lobbying literature seems to be highly relevant for a small member state's performance in EU decision-making. The hypotheses, which originated from the lobbying scholarship, have been fully or partially confirmed in the Czech case. The early warning strategies loom relatively large in the activity of Czech representatives and the case studies showed that acquiring insider status helps enormously in pushing the country's position through. While the concept of small states as lobbyists is not new in the academic literature, this book has shown that the concept can be used to generate testable hypotheses and to provide an original perspective for the study of state behaviour in the EU. While some of the contextual factors that the lobbying literature emphasizes have not been confirmed as relevant here, such as the institutional framework, others have proven to be significant, particularly issue salience and motivation.

Second, the research has shown how the combination of constructivist (long-term Europeanization) and rational-choice (issue-specific interest promotion) approaches can be combined. On one hand, the case studies revealed what the rational-choice scholars expect, namely an *ex ante* definition of national priorities on a particular issue and subsequent engagement at the European level, which aims at maximizing a country's gains. On the other hand, the survey confirmed the expectations of constructivist scholars that EU membership leads to a change in behaviour. In addition, the revealed discrepancy between the civil servants and the political elite, whom the civil servants blame for hampering their work by not defining consistent priorities, suggests that a stronger socialization – or Brusselization (cf. Juncos and

Pomorska, 2011) – has taken place among the public administration than among politicians.

It has been confirmed that learning takes place during the member state's membership, which leads to the adjustment of the methods that the country's representatives use to promote national positions in the Council. The survey respondents have collectively identified as important exactly those methods that the theory expects to be the most effective for a small state, particularly the specialization and expertise that constitute the core of the insider status. However, these methods have only been partially used in practice by the Czech representatives. One possible lesson for the literature may be that learning needs more time than just a decade and that the Czech Republic is currently in the stage where it has been able to understand what is necessary, but unable to put the knowledge into effect.

The rest of the findings, however, lead to another interpretation of the current situation, namely to the identification of factors that curb the speed of the learning process at the institutional level. First, there is the human resources issue. The Czech Republic has apparently been unable to embrace the arguably most Brusselized individuals within the public administration. An extremely high percentage of officials with Brussels experience do not contribute to the formulation of Czech European policy. Since the whole socialization idea is based on the change of the ideas and identities of individuals who are the means of transformation of the whole institutions, the absence of such individuals or their limited number can naturally cause the process of institutional change to slow down. With a high probability, the missing Civil Service Act has contributed significantly to this situation. The fact that the act has now been in force since July 2015 could lead to a lower number of officials leaving the EU agenda or the public administration after their tenure in Brussels and in turn speed up the process of institutional change. This will, however, have to be tested in a couple of years, because it is too early to collect any reasonable data at the moment. Second, the lack of political priorities constitutes an objective obstacle to the implementation of the "learning". In this respect, the learning itself would not be limited (the Czech Republic equated with the public administration has learned how to navigate in the EU), but it would hit the limits of what the Czech Republic (as an actor consisting of the public administration implementing political assignments) can do.

In the Czech case, the combination of both reasons seems to be at the heart of the problem. Democracy and human rights policy, where the Czech Republic has been able to acquire insider status, may serve as a counterexample: there is personal continuity ensuring that the lessons learned are reflected in the subsequent practice. Unlike other working groups studied here, the COHOM was for most of its existence composed of representatives sent from the capitals. The Czech member has, exceptionally, been with COHOM for the whole decade and was, at the same time, the desk officer responsible for drafting of bulk of the positions for the working group. In addition, support for democracy and human rights has been one of the few priorities shared among all political leaders of the Foreign Ministry, although with some differences in the wording and preferences within the issue since 2014.

As a result, this confirms the claims in the literature that social learning in general and Europeanization in particular do not necessarily lead to convergence, to everybody doing things the same way (cf. Vink and Graziano, 2007: 10). The quality and results of the political debate and human resources policy are examples of factors that have an effect on the behaviour of a member state in the EU and the methods that the state representatives in the Council employ.

What does the Czech case say about other member states?

It is naturally highly problematic to generalize from a single case, unless the case is methodologically determined and used for limited purposes, such as various types of crucial cases that are suitable for disproving a theory (cf. Gerring, 2008). The Czech Republic is no such case in this book and the aim was to use the Czech example as a case that would suggest possible directions for future research. At the same time, there is some room for tentative claims about what the Czech case suggests for other EU member states.

The Czech case suggests that the length of membership is not the crucial factor for a small state to employ various methods of interest promotion effectively. Other elements have a huge impact on the country's performance, notably the stability of the public administration and effective work with human resources, and stable and predictable priorities. This helps understand why many of the small member states that are regularly referred to as influential could have been EU members for relatively short periods of time, most notably Sweden. It also offers an alternative perspective on the performance of the so-called new member states. Generally, their influence within the EU has been considered relatively limited. This may, however, be the result not of the short membership, but of the fact that many of these countries have been struggling with administrative reform, low quality of public debate, and a polarized political scene. Thus, expecting the Czech Republic or Hungary to be as successful in promoting national priorities in EU polices as the Netherlands or Sweden in a few years, as soon as they learn how to pull the strings, is probably a grave mistake. Unless the countries define their national priorities more clearly and in a more inclusive manner, increase the predictability of their positions, and stabilize (and depoliticize) their public administrations, they will inevitably punch below their weight.

At the same time, the scepticism about the new member states' ability to engage in more sophisticated methods of interest promotion does not imply that these countries are completely unable to promote their positions in a more elaborate manner. There can be pockets of excellence and stability in which they can perform well in the same way that the Czech Republic managed to become an insider on the issue of election observation within the broader support of democracy and human rights. These pockets are, however, doomed to remain just that – exceptions to the overall performance – if the countries continue in the current trend of political polarization and politicization of public administration, which we have recently seen most clearly in Hungary and in Poland.

Opportunities for further research

The insight into the methods for interest promotion presented in this book suggests that lobbying literature can inspire new perspectives on analysis of EU decision-making. The categorization of methods used here is just one of them and there are many other concepts that seem relevant for the EU-related research. The concept of 'managing the home front' (van Schendelen, 2010: 199), which suggests that there is a link between lobbying performance and the ability to coordinate the various actors that present the position, may serve as an example. While parts of the home front have been studied extensively in the form of EU policy coordination, they have been largely restricted to the state administration. The home front should, however, be understood much more broadly, including political parties, business, and other non-state actors.

This book has shown how the Czech Republic has embraced early warning methods as an important part of its Council activities. Future research should dig into this early warning and try to unpack how and if the timely information changes the subsequent behaviour of a small state and whether some early warning methods are more important than others. The same could be done for the methods that lead to insider status and, more generally, to a more thorough analysis of the concept of insider, i.e. are there different types of insiders, do all insiders have comparable influence?

While this research on the Czech Republic has been limited by its focus on a single member state, larger comparative research is needed to test the lobbying-inspired hypotheses more thoroughly. It has been shown here that the length of membership is apparently not the crucial variable when assessing the spectrum of methods that member states employ to advance their interests; rather the stability and predictability of the political debate and the human resources management in the public administration are important. A cross-policy comparison cannot offer a conclusive judgement on this hypothesis. A cross-country research design would be necessary, for example comprising two or more countries with different administrative traditions and the same length of EU membership.

When and under which conditions are small member states able to promote their interests across various EU institutions? Although foreign policy is not a particularly good area to study the engagement of the European Commission and the European Parliament in a member state's strategy, the case studies presented above suggest that the Czech Republic has not been very keen on and capable of reaching out to the other institutions, even on issues where they could make a difference. Is this just a question of limited capacities and manpower and there are simply not enough officials at small member states' permanent representations to handle the additional agenda? Do other small member states have similar problems or are they able to reach out more effectively?

This book has focused on external relations only, while other accounts have covered just economic policies (cf. Panke, 2010b). The comparison of the two remains a big question for future research: to what extent does the small states' interest promotion differ in internal market-related policies and in foreign affairs. While foreign policy may be considered marginal for a small member state sometimes, the internal market is clearly salient irrespective of the size. The political debate and the political interest in successful promotion of the country's position should thus be much more focused and the priorities much more clearly defined. This research suggested that higher policy salience does indeed lead to higher frequency of the use of all types of interest promotion methods. Arguably, the high salience of the internal market should signify very high activity on the part of the small state negotiators.

Finally, this book has deliberately avoided the question of success. It has expected, in line with the lobbying literature, that the more sophisticated methods are more likely to lead to success in interest promotion. But this needs to be tested in the context of small EU states and the results need to be confronted with the large existing body of literature that has studied success in EU negotiations. As a result, elaborate research designs that would be able to control for contextual factors would be needed to test to what extent small states should learn from private interest advocates how to make their point in the Council more efficiently and more successfully.

Interviews

Interview #1:	Czech Permanent Representation to the EU; Brussels, 16 May 2011
Interview #2:	Danish Permanent Representation to the EU; Brussels, 12 December 2013
Interview #3:	Danish Permanent Representation to the EU; Brussels, 12 December 2013
Interview #4:	Czech Permanent Representation to the EU; Brussels, 12 December 2013
Interview #5:	Czech Permanent Representation to the EU; Brussels, 12 December 2013
Interview #6:	Swedish Permanent Representation to the EU; Brussels, 13 December 2013
Interview #7:	Czech Permanent Representation to the EU; Brussels, 13 December 2013
Interview #8:	Czech Permanent Representation to the EU; Brussels, 13 December 2013
Interview #9:	Czech Ministry of Foreign Affairs; Prague, 2 January 2014
Interview #10:	Czech Ministry of Foreign Affairs; Prague, 2 January 2014
Interview #11:	European Commission, DG ELARG; Brussels, 3 April 2014
Interview #12:	Czech Ministry of Industry and Trade; Prague, 14 May 2014
Interview #13:	Czech Ministry of Industry and Trade; Prague, 19 May 2014
Interview #14:	European External Action Service; Brussels, 20 May 2014
Interview #15:	Czech Permanent Representation to the EU; Brussels, 20 May 2014
Interview #16:	Czech Permanent Representation to the EU; Brussels, 20 May 2014
Interview #17:	European Commission, DG TRADE; Brussels, 20 May 2014
Interview #18:	European Commission, DG TRADE; Brussels, 20 May 2014
Interview #19:	Finnish Permanent Representation to the EU; Brussels, 21 May 2014
Interview #20:	European External Action Service; Brussels, 21 May 2014

118 *Interviews*

Interview #21:	European Parliament, INTA Secretariat; Brussels, 21 May 2014
Interview #22:	Czech Ministry of Foreign Affairs; Prague, 28 May 2014
Interview #23:	Czech Ministry of Foreign Affairs; Prague, 28 May 2014
Interview #24:	Czech Ministry of Foreign Affairs; Prague, 11 June 2014
Interview #25:	Czech Ministry of Foreign Affairs; Prague, 24 June 2014
Interview #26:	Czech Ministry of Foreign Affairs; Prague, 27 June 2014
Interview #27:	European Commission, DG DEVCO; Brussels, 30 June 2014
Interview #28:	Czech Permanent Representation to the EU; Brussels, 1 July 2014
Interview #29:	Czech Permanent Representation to the EU; Brussels, 1 July 2014
Interview #30:	Polish Permanent Representation to the EU; Brussels, 1 July 2014
Interview #31:	European External Action Service; Brussels, 1 July 2014
Interview #32:	European Commission, DG ELARG; Brussels, 1 July 2014
Interview #33:	General Secretariat of the Council; Brussels, 1 July 2014
Interview #34:	European Commission, DG DEVCO; Brussels, 2 July 2014
Interview #35:	European External Action Service; Brussels, 2 July 2014
Interview #36:	European External Action Service; Brussels, 2 July 2014
Interview #37:	French Permanent Representation to the EU; Brussels, 3 July 2014
Interview #38:	Czech Permanent Representation to the EU; Brussels, 3 July 2014
Interview #39:	Czech Ministry of Industry and Trade; telephone, 21 August 2014
Interview #40:	Czech Ministry of Foreign Affairs; Prague, 24 November 2014
Interview #41:	Czech Permanent Representation to the EU; Brussels, 4 December 2014
Interview #42:	Dutch Permanent Representation to the EU; Brussels, 5 December 2014
Interview #43:	European External Action Service; Brussels, 5 December 2014
Interview #44:	Czech Ministry of Foreign Affairs; telephone, 22 January 2015
Interview #45:	Czech Permanent Representation to the EU; telephone, 30 July 2015
Interview #46:	Czech Ministry of Industry and Trade; Prague, 4 August 2015
Interview #47:	Czech Ministry of Interior; email, 4 August 2015
Interview #48:	Czech Ministry of Foreign Affairs; Prague, 27 August 2015
Interview #48:	Czech Ministry of Foreign Affairs; Prague, 4 September 2015
Interview #50:	European Commission, DG DEVCO; telephone, 1 October 2015

Interview #51: European Commission, DG DEVCO; telephone, 8 October 2015
Interview #52: Election Observation and Democratic Support; telephone, 13 October 2015
Interview #53: Czech Permanent Representation to the EU; telephone, 15 October 2015
Interview #54: Democracy Reporting International; telephone, 19 October 2015

Bibliography

Archer C and Nugent N (2002) Introduction: Small States and the European Union. *Current Politics and Economics of Europe* 11(1): 1–10.
Arter D (2000) Small State Influence within the EU: The Case of Finland's 'Northern Dimension Initiative'. *Journal of Common Market Studies* 38(5): 677–697.
Axt H-J, Milososki A, and Schwarz O (2007) Europäisierung: Ein weites Feld – Literaturbericht und Forschungsfragen. *Politische Vierteljahresschrift* 48(1): 136–149.
Bache I and Marshall A (2004) Europeanisation and Domestic Change: A Governance Approach to Institutional Adaptation in Britain. *Queen's Papers on Europeanization* 5/2004.
Baldacchino G (2009) Thucydides or Kissinger? A Critical Review of Smaller State Diplomacy. In: Cooper AF and Shaw TM (eds), *The Diplomacies of Small States: Between Vulnerability and Resilience*, International Political Economy Series. Basingstoke: Palgrave Macmillan, pp. 21–40.
Balzacq T and Carrera S (eds) (2006) *Security versus Freedom? A Challenge for Europe's Future*. Aldershot: Ashgate.
Bardakçı M (2010) EU Engagement in Conflict Resolution in Georgia: Towards a More Proactive Role. *Caucasian Review of International Affairs* 4(3): 214–236.
Bartovic V (2008) Limited Resources, Global Ambitions: The Czech Republic's Democracy Assistance Policies and Priorities. In: Kucharczyk J and Lovitt J (eds), *Democracy's New Champions: European Democracy Assistance after EU Enlargement*. Prague: PASOS, pp. 29–49.
Baumgartner FR and Mahoney C (2008) The Two Faces of Framing: Individual-Level Framing and Collective Issue Definition in the European Union. *European Union Politics* 9(3): 435–449.
Baumgartner FR, Berry JM, Hojnacki M, et al. (2009) *Lobbying and Policy Change: Who Wins, Who Loses, and Why*. Chicago and London: University of Chicago Press.
Beisbart C, Bovens L, and Hartmann S (2005) A Utilitarian Assessment of Alternative Decision Rules in the Council of Ministers. *European Union Politics* 6(4): 395–418.
Beneš V and Braun M (2010) Evropský rozměr české zahraniční politiky. In: Kořan M (ed.), *Česká zahraniční politika v roce 2009*. Praha: Ústav mezinárodních vztahů, pp. 61–87.
Beyers J and Trondal J (2004) How Nation States 'Hit' Europe: Ambiguity and Representation in the European Union. *West European Politics* 27(5): 919–942.
Björkdahl A (2008) Norm Advocacy: A Small State Strategy to Influence the EU. *Journal of European Public Policy* 15(1): 135–154.

Bloomfield J, Copsey N, Mayhew A, et al. (2011) *Local and Regional Dimensions of the European Neighbourhood Policy: An Overview of the Role of the Committee of the Regions*. Brussels: European Union.
Bomberg E and Peterson J (2000) Policy Transfer and Europeanization: Passing the Heineken Test? *Queen's Papers on Europeanization* 2/2000.
Börzel TA (2002) Pace-Setting, Foot-Dragging, and Fence-Sitting: Member State Responses to Europeanization. *Journal of Common Market Studies* 40(2): 193–214.
Börzel TA (2003) Shaping and Taking EU Policies: Member State Responses to Europeanization. *Queen's Papers on Europeanization* 2/2003.
Börzel TA and Risse T (2000) When Europe Hits Home: Europeanization and Domestic Change. *European Integration Online Papers* 4(15).
Börzel TA and Risse T (2003) Conceptualizing the Domestic Impact of Europe. In: Featherstone K and Radaelli CM (eds), *The Politics of Europeanization*. Oxford: Oxford University Press, pp. 57–80.
Bouwen P and Mccown M (2007) Lobbying versus Litigation: Political and Legal Strategies of Interest Representation in the European Union. *Journal of European Public Policy* 14(3): 422–443.
Brusenbauch Meislová M (2012) *Evropeizace české zahraniční rozvojové spolupráce*. Olomouc: Univerzita Palackého v Olomouci.
Bulmer S (2007) Theorizing Europeanization. In: Graziano P and Vink MP (eds), *Europeanization: New Research Agendas*. Basingstoke: Palgrave Macmillan, pp. 46–58.
Bulmer S and Radaelli CM (2004) The Europeanisation of National Policy? *Queen's Papers on Europeanization* 1/2004.
Bulmer S, Dolowitz D, Humphreys P, et al. (2007) *Policy Transfer in European Union Governance: Regulating the Utilities*. Abingdon and New York: Routledge.
Bunse S (2009) *Small States and EU Governance: Leadership through the Council Presidency*. Basingstoke: Palgrave Macmillan.
Cameron F (2012) *An Introduction to European Foreign Policy*. Abingdon and New York: Routledge.
Caporaso JA (2007) The Three Worlds of Regional Integration Theory. In: Graziano P and Vink MP (eds), *Europeanization: New Research Agendas*. Basingstoke: Palgrave Macmillan, pp. 23–34.
Carothers T (1997) The Observers Observed. *Journal of Democracy* 8(3): 17–31.
Carrubba CJ and Volden C (2001) Explaining Institutional Change in the European Union: What Determines the Voting Rule in the Council of Ministers? *European Union Politics* 2(1): 5–30.
Chalmers AW (2011) Interests, Influence and Information: Comparing the Influence of Interest Groups in the European Union. *Journal of European Integration* 33(4): 471–486.
Checkel JT (2005) International Institutions and Socialization in Europe: Introduction and Framework. *International Organization* 59(4): 801–826.
Coen D (2007) Empirical and Theoretical Studies in EU Lobbying. *Journal of European Public Policy* 14(3): 333–345.
Conway M and Patel KK (eds) (2010) *Europeanization in the Twentieth Century: Historical Approaches*. Basingstoke: Palgrave Macmillan.
Copsey N and Pomorska K (2014) The Influence of Newer Member States in the European Union: The Case of Poland and the Eastern Partnership. *Europe-Asia Studies* 66(3): 421–443.

Costello R and Thomson R (2013) The Distribution of Power among EU Institutions: Who Wins under Codecision and Why? *Journal of European Public Policy* 20(7): 1025–1039.

Council of the European Union (1994) Council Regulation (EC) No. 3281/94 of 19 December 1994 applying a four-year scheme of generalized tariff preferences (1995 to 1998) in respect of certain industrial products originating in developing countries. *OJ L* 348, 31.12.1994, p. 1.

Council of the European Union (2005) Council Regulation (EC) No 980/2005 of 27 June 2005 applying a scheme of generalised tariff preferences. *OJ L* 169, 30.6.2005, p. 1.

Council of the European Union (2008) Council Joint Action 2008/736/CFSP of 15 September 2008 on the European Union Monitoring Mission in Georgia, EUMM Georgia. *OJ L* 248, 17.9.2008, p. 26.

Council of the European Union (2012) *EU Strategic Framework and Action Plan on Human Rights and Democracy*. 11855/12. Luxembourg.

Council of the European Union (2013) Council Decision 2013/446/CFSP of 6 September 2013 amending Decision 2010/452/CFSP on the European Union Monitoring Mission in Georgia, EUMM Georgia. *OJ L* 240, 7.9.2013, p. 21.

Council of the European Union (2014) Council Decision 2014/915/CFSP of 16 December 2014 amending Decision 2010/452/CFSP on the European Union Monitoring Mission in Georgia, EUMM Georgia. *OJ L* 360, 17.12.2014, p. 56.

Cremona M and Hillion C (2006) L'Union fait la force? Potential and Limitations of the European Neighbourhood Policy as an Integrated EU Foreign and Security Policy. *EUI Working Papers* (Law No. 2006/39).

Czech Statistical Office (2013) *Czech Republic in 2012*. Prague: Czech Statistical Office.

Damro C (2012) Market Power Europe. *Journal of European Public Policy* 19(5): 682–699.

Dangerfield M (2014) V4: A New Brand for Europe? Ten Years of Post-Accession Regional Cooperation in Central Europe. *Poznan University of Economics Review* 14(4): 71–90.

Davis Cross MK (2010) Cooperation by Committee: The EU Military Committee and the Committee for Civilian Crisis Management. *EU ISS Occasional Paper* 82.

de Flers NA and Müller P (2012) Dimensions and Mechanisms of the Europeanization of Member State Foreign Policy: State of the Art and New Research Avenues. *Journal of European Integration* 34(1): 19–35.

De Ville F and Orbie J (2011) The European Union's Trade Policy Response to the Crisis: Paradigm Lost or Reinforced? *European Integration Online Papers* 15(2): 1–22.

Dos Santos NB, Farias R, and Cunha R (2005) Generalized System of Preferences in General Agreement on Tariffs and Trade/World Trade Organization: History and Current Issues. *Journal of World Trade* 39(4): 637–670.

Drulák P (2010) Comparing the EU Presidencies: A Pragmatic Perspective. In: Drulák P and Šabič Z (eds), *The Czech and Slovenian EU Presidencies in a Comparative Perspective*. Dordrecht: Republic of Letters Publishing, pp. 1–19.

Drulák P and Braun M (eds) (2010) *The Quest for the National Interest: A Methodological Reflection on Czech Foreign Policy*. Frankfurt am Main: Peter Lang.

Drulák P and Handl V (eds) (2010) *Hledání českých zájmů: Vnitřní rozmanitost a vnější akceschopnost*. Praha: Ústav mezinárodních vztahů.

Drulák P and Horký O (eds) (2010) *Hledání českých zájmů: Obchod, lidská práva a mezinárodní rozvoj*. Praha: Ústav mezinárodních vztahů.

Drulák P and Stříteký V (eds) (2010) *Hledání českých zájmů: Mezinárodní bezpečnost.* Praha: Ústav mezinárodních vztahů.
Duke S (2009) Consensus Building in ESDP: The Lessons of Operation Artemis. *International Politics* 46(4): 398–412.
Dwan R (2005) Civilian Tasks and Capabilities in EU Operations. In: Glasius M and Kaldor M (eds), *A Human Security Doctrine for Europe: Project, Principles, Practicalities.* London: Routledge, pp. 264–289.
Edwards G (2006) The New Member States and the Making of EU Foreign Policy. *European Foreign Affairs Review* 11(2): 143–162.
EEAS (2014) *Strategic Review of EUMM Georgia.* 9209/14 (not public). Brussels.
EEAS (2015a) All the missions. Available from: http://eeas.europa.eu/eueom/missions/index_en.htm.
EEAS (2015b) EUMM Georgia: Facts and Figures. Available from: www.eumm.eu/en/about_eumm/facts_and_figures.
Elgström O and Jönsson C (2000) Negotiation in the European Union: Bargaining or Problem-Solving? *Journal of European Public Policy* 7(5): 684–704.
European Commission (2000) *Communication from the Commission on EU Election Assistance and Observation.* COM (2000) 191 final. Brussels: European Commission.
European Commission (2003) *Communication from the Commission to the Council and the European Parliament: Wider Europe – Neighbourhood: A New Framework for Relations with our Eastern and Southern Neighbours.* COM (2003) 104 final. Brussels: European Commission.
European Commission (2006a) *EC Methodological Guide on Electoral Assistance.* Brussels: European Commission.
European Commission (2006b) *Global Europe: Competing in the World – A Contribution to the EU's Growth and Jobs Strategy.* COM (2006) 567 final. Brussels: European Commission.
European Commission (2008) *Handbook for European Union Election Observation.* Brussels: European Commission.
European Commission (2010a) *Communication from the Commission to the European Parliament and the Council: Taking Stock of the European Neighbourhood Policy.* COM (2010) 207. Brussels: European Commission.
European Commission (2010b) *Trade, Growth and World Affairs: Trade Policy as a Core Component of the EU's 2020 Strategy.* COM (2010) 612 final. Brussels: European Commission.
European Commission (2011a) *Draft Commission Decision on the Annual Action Programme 2011 for the European Instrument for the promotion of Democracy and Human Rights worldwide (EIDHR) to be financed under Articles 19 04 01 and 19 04 03 of the general budget of the European Union.* Available from: www.eidhr.eu/files/dmfile/annual-action-programme-2011_en.pdf.
European Commission (2011b) *EU Response to the Arab Spring: The SPRING Programme.* MEMO/11/636. Brussels: European Commission.
European Commission (2011c) *Executive Summary of the Impact Assessment Accompanying the Document Proposal for a Regulation of the European Parliament and of the Council on Applying a Scheme of Generalised Tariff Preferences.* SEC (2011) 537 final. Brussels: European Commission.
European Commission (2011d) *Impact Assessment Accompanying the Document Regulation of the European Parliament and of the Council Laying down General*

Provisions Establishing a European Neighbourhood Instrument. SEC (2011) 1466 final. Brussels: European Commission.

European Commission (2011e) *More Benefits from Preferential Trade Tariffs for Countries Most in Need: Reform of the EU Generalised System of Preferences*. MEMO/11/284. Brussels: European Commission.

European Commission (2011f) *Proposal for a Regulation of the European Parliament and of the Council Applying a Scheme of Generalised Tariff Preferences*. COM (2011) 241 final. Brussels: European Commission.

European Commission (2011g) *Proposal for a Regulation of the European Parliament and of the Council Establishing a European Neighbourhood Instrument*. COM (2011) 839 final. Brussels: European Commission.

European Commission (2011h) *Proposal for a Regulation of the European Parliament and of the Council Establishing a Financing Instrument for Democracy and Human Rights Worldwide*. COM (2011) 844 final. Brussels: European Commission.

European Commission (2012) *Enhanced Cooperation in the Eastern Partnership: The Eastern Partnership Integration and Cooperation (EaPIC) Programme*. MEMO/12/491. Brussels: European Commission.

European Commission (2014) *Publication of Preliminary Data on 2013 Official Development Assistance*. MEMO/14/263. Brussels: European Commission.

European Commission (2015) *Public Opinion in the European Union: Standard Eurobarometer 83 (First Results)*. Brussels: European Commission.

European Commission and High Representative of the Union for Foreign Affairs and Security Policy (2011a) *Joint Communication to the European Council, European Parliament, the Council, the European Economic and Social Committee and the Committee of Regions: A Partnership for Democracy and Shared Prosperity with the Southern Mediterranean*. COM (2011) 200 final. Brussels.

European Commission and High Representative of the Union for Foreign Affairs and Security Policy (2011b) *Joint Communication to the European Parliament, the Council, the European Economic and Social Committee and the Committee of Regions: A New Response to a Changing Neighbourhood*. COM (2011) 303 final. Brussels.

European Commission and High Representative of the Union for Foreign Affairs and Security Policy (2012a) *Joint Communication to the European Parliament, the Council, the European Economic and Social Committee and the Committee of Regions: Delivering on a new European Neighbourhood Policy*. JOIN (2012) 14 final. Brussels.

European Commission and High Representative of the Union for Foreign Affairs and Security Policy (2012b) *Joint Report to the European Parliament, the Council, the European Economic and Social Committee and the Committee of Regions: Implementation of the Agenda for Action on Democracy Support in the EU's External Relations*. JOIN (2012) 28 final. Brussels.

European Commission and High Representative of the Union for Foreign Affairs and Security Policy (2013) *Joint Communication to the European Parliament and the Council: The EU's Comprehensive Approach to External Conflict and Crises*. JOIN (2013) 30 final. Brussels.

European Council (2013) *Conclusions*. EUCO 217/13. Brussels.

European Parliament (2011) *Minutes of INTA Meeting of 20 December 2011*. INTA_PV(2011)1220_1. Brussels.

European Parliament (2012) *Minutes of the EP Plenary of 11 June 2012*. PV 11/06/2012 - 19. Strasbourg.

European Parliament (2013a) *European Parliament Legislative Resolution of 11 December 2013 on the Proposal for a Regulation of the European Parliament and of the Council Establishing a European Neighbourhood Instrument*. P7_TA(2013)0567. Strasbourg.

European Parliament (2013b) *European Parliament Legislative Resolution of 11 December 2013 on the Proposal for a Regulation of the European Parliament and of the Council Establishing a Financing Instrument for the Promotion of Democracy and Human Rights Worldwide*. P7_TA(2013)0570. Strasbourg.

European Parliament and Council (2012) Regulation (EU) No 978/2012 of the European Parliament and of the Council of 25 October 2012 applying a scheme of generalised tariff preferences and repealing Council Regulation (EC) No 732/2008. *OJ L* 303, 31.10.2012, p. 1.

European Parliament and Council (2014a) Regulation (EU) No 232/2014 of the European Parliament and of the Council of 11 March 2014 establishing a European Neighbourhood Instrument. *OJ L* 77, 15.3.2014, p. 27.

European Parliament and Council (2014b) Regulation (EU) No 235/2014 of the European Parliament and of the Council of 11 March 2014 establishing a financing instrument for democracy and human rights worldwide. *OJ L* 77, 15.3.2014, p. 85.

Faist T and Ette A (eds) (2007) *The Europeanization of National Policies and Politics of Immigration: Between Autonomy and the European Union*. Basingstoke: Palgrave Macmillan.

Fawn R (2006) Battle over the Box: International Election Observation Missions, Political Competition and Retrenchment in the post-Soviet Space. *International Affairs* 82(6): 1133–1153.

Fiala P, Hloušek V, and Krpec O (2007) Evropeizace českých odborových svazů: proměny strategie reprezentace zájmů a okruhu partnerů v procesu evropské integrace. *Politologický časopis* 14(2): 95–109.

Fiott D (ed.) (2015) *The Common Security and Defence Policy: National Perspectives*, Egmont Paper. Ghent: Academia Press.

Fischer S (2009) EUMM Georgia. In: Grevi G, Helly D, and Keohane D (eds), *ESDP: The First 10 Years (1999–2009)*. Paris: EU ISS, pp. 379–390.

Fontana M-C (2011) Europeanization and Domestic Policy Concertation: How Actors Use Europe to Modify Domestic Patterns of Policy-Making. *Journal of European Public Policy* 18(5): 654–671.

Foreign and Commonwealth Office (2014) *Explanatory Memorandum on the European Union's Common Foreign and Security Policy: Council Decision Amending Decision 2010/452/CFSP on the European Union Monitoring Mission in Georgia, EUMM Georgia*. London: Foreign and Commonwealth Office.

Freire MR and Simão L (2013) The EU's Security Actorness: The Case of EUMM in Georgia. *European Security* 22(4): 464–477.

Gabriel M, Matúš A, and Bystrický R (2011) *Final Report: Implementation of One of the Recommendations of the EU Election Observation Mission in Sierra Leone 2007*. Bratislava: Občianske oko.

Gasiorek M (2010) *Mid-term Evaluation of the EU's Generalised System of Preferences*. Brighton: CARIS. Available from: http://trade.ec.europa.eu/doclib/docs/2010/may/tradoc_146196.pdf.

Gaspers J (2008) The Quest for European Foreign Policy Consistency and the Treaty of Lisbon. *Humanitas Journal of European Studies* 2(1): 19–53.

Gauttier P (2004) Horizontal Coherence and the External Competences of the European Union. *European Law Journal* 10(1): 23–41.

Gebhard C (2009) The Crisis Management and Planning Directorate: Recalibrating ESDP Planning and Conduct Capacities. *CFSP Forum* 7(4): 8–14.

Gerring J (2008) Case Selection for Case-Study Analysis: Qualitative and Quantitative Techniques. In: Box-Steffensmeier JM, Brady HE, and Collier D (eds), *The Oxford Handbook of Political Methodology*. Oxford: Oxford University Press, pp. 645–684.

Golub J (2012) How the European Union Does Not Work: National Bargaining Success in the Council of Ministers. *Journal of European Public Policy* 19(9): 1294–1315.

Government of the Czech Republic (1996) *Programové prohlášení vlády*. Praha.

Government of the Czech Republic (1999) *Koncepce zahraniční politiky České republiky*. Praha.

Government of the Czech Republic (2003) *Koncepce zahraniční politiky České republiky na léta 2003–2006*. Praha.

Government of the Czech Republic (2009) *Work Programme of the Czech Presidency: Europe without Barriers*. Prague. Available from: www.eu2009.cz/assets/news-and-documents/news/cz-pres_programme_en.pdf.

Government of the Czech Republic (2010) *Konsolidované úplně znění Statutu vládního zmocněnce pro zastupování České republiky před Soudním dvorem Evropské unie ve znění usnesení vlády č. 113 ze dne 4. února 2004 a usnesení č. 382 ze dne 24. května 2010*. Praha.

Government of the Czech Republic (2011a) *Koncepce zahraniční politiky České republiky*. Praha.

Government of the Czech Republic (2011b) *Security Strategy of the Czech Republic*. Prague.

Government of the Czech Republic (2014a) *Směrnice vlády o postupu při nakládání s dokumenty Rady a jinými dokumenty Evropské unie, projednávání záležitostí Evropské unie v Senátu a Poslanecké sněmovně Parlamentu České republiky a přípravě českého jazykového znění právních aktů*. Praha.

Government of the Czech Republic (2014b) *Statut Výboru pro Evropskou unii*. Praha.

Government of the Czech Republic (2015a) *Concept of the Czech Republic's Foreign Policy*. Prague.

Government of the Czech Republic (2015b) *Koncepce politiky ČR v EU: Aktivní a srozumitelná ČR v jednotné Evropě*. Praha.

Government of the Czech Republic (2015c) *Security Strategy of the Czech Republic*. Prague.

Government of the Czech Republic (2015d) *Účast členů vlády na jednáních Rady EU se meziročně zvýšila*. Available from: www.vlada.cz/cz/media-centrum/aktualne/ucast-clenu-vlady-na-jednanich-rady-eu-se-mezirocne-zvysila-128151.

Graziano P and Vink MP (eds) (2007) *Europeanization: New Research Agendas*. Basingstoke: Palgrave Macmillan.

Greenwood J (2011) *Interest Representation in the European Union*. Basingstoke: Palgrave Macmillan.

Gross E (2008) *EU and the Comprehensive Approach*, DIIS Report. Copenhagen: Danish Institute for International Studies.

Häge FM (2010) Politicising Council Decision-Making: The Effect of European Parliament Empowerment. *West European Politics* 34(1): 18–47.

Hall PA and Taylor RCR (1996) Political Science and the Three New Institutionalisms. *Political Studies* 44: 936–957.

Handl V (2009) Česká politika vůči Spolkové republice Německo: od normalizace k evropeizaci. In: Kořan M (ed.), *Česká zahraniční politika v zrcadle sociálně-vědního výzkumu*. Praha: Ústav mezinárodních vztahů, pp. 19–43.

Haverland M and Liefferink D (2012) Member State Interest Articulation in the Commission Phase: Institutional Pre-Conditions for Influencing 'Brussels'. *Journal of European Public Policy* 19(2): 179–197.

Hayes-Renshaw F (2009) Least Accessible But Not Inaccessible: Lobbying the Council and the European Council. In: Coen D and Richardson J (eds), *Lobbying the European Union: Institutions, Actors, and Issues*, Oxford: Oxford University Press, pp. 70–88.

Hayes-Renshaw F and Wallace H (2006) *The Council of Ministers*. Basingstoke: Palgrave Macmillan.

Heisenberg D (2005) The Institution of 'Consensus' in the European Union: Formal versus Informal Decision-Making in the Council. *European Journal of Political Research* 44(1): 65–90.

Helly D (2009) EUFOR Tchad/RCA. In: Grevi G, Helly D, and Keohane D (eds), *ESDP: The First 10 Years (1999–2009)*. Paris: EU ISS, pp. 339–351.

Héritier A (ed.) (2001) *Differential Europe: The European Union Impact on National Policymaking*. Lanham, MD: Rowman & Littlefield.

Hermann MG, Preston T, Korany B, et al. (2001) Who Leads Matters: The Effects of Powerful Individuals. *International Studies Review* 3(2): 83–131.

Hertz R and Leuffen D (2011) Group Size and Formalization: A Comparison of European Union Decision-Making before and after Eastern Enlargement. *Geopolitics, History and International Relations* 3(1): 59–76.

Hey JAK (2003) Introducing Small State Foreign Policy. In: Hey JAK (ed.), *Small States in World Politics: Explaining Foreign Policy Behavior*. Boulder, CO: Lynne Rienner Publishers, pp. 1–11.

Hix S and Høyland B (2011) *The Political System of the European Union*. Basingstoke: Palgrave Macmillan.

Hloušek V and Pšeja P (2008) Evropeizace politických stran a stranického systému v České republice. *Politologický časopis* 15(4): 299–317.

Hollis R (2012) No Friend of Democratization: Europe's Role in the Genesis of the 'Arab Spring'. *International Affairs* 88(1): 81–94.

Hooghe L and Marks G (2001) *Multi-Level Governance and European Integration*. Lanham, MD: Rowman & Littlefield.

Hosli MO (1996) Coalitions and Power: Effects of Qualified Majority Voting in the Council of the European Union. *Journal of Common Market Studies* 34(2): 255–273.

Hosli MO, Mattila M, and Uriot M (2011) Voting in the Council of the European Union after the 2004 Enlargement: A Comparison of Old and New Member States. *Journal of Common Market Studies* 49(6): 1249–1270.

Howell KE (2009) Europeanization, Globalization and Domestication: Financial Services Regulation in the UK. *International Journal of Law and Management* 51(5): 310–326.

Hughes J, Sasse G, and Gordon C (eds) (2005) *Europeanization and Regionalization in the EU's Enlargement to Central and Eastern Europe: The Myth of Conditionality*. Basingstoke: Palgrave Macmillan.

Hula KW (1999) *Lobbying Together: Interest Group Coalitions in Legislative Politics*. Washington, DC: Georgetown University Press.

Hynek N and Střítecký V (2010a) Český diskurz o protiraketové obraně ve světle reflexe národního zájmu. *Mezinárodní vztahy* 45(1): 5–32.

Hynek N and Střítecký V (2010b) The Rise and Fall of the Third Site of Ballistic Missile Defense. *Communist and Post-Communist Studies* 43(2): 179–187.

Irondelle B (2003) Europeanization without the European Union? French Military Reforms 1991–96. *Journal of European Public Policy* 10(2): 208–226.

Jakobsen PV (2006) The ESDP and Civilian Rapid Reaction: Adding Value Is Harder than Expected. *European Security* 15(3): 299–321.

Jakobsen PV (2009) Small States, Big Influence: The Overlooked Nordic Influence on the Civilian ESDP. *Journal of Common Market Studies* 47(1): 81–102.

Joos K (2011) *Lobbying in the New Europe: Successful Representation of Interests after the Treaty of Lisbon*. Weinheim: Wiley-VCH.

Juncos AE and Pomorska K (2006) Playing the Brussels Game: Strategic Socialisation in the CFSP Council Working Groups. *European Integration online Papers* 10(11).

Juncos AE and Pomorska K (2007) The Deadlock That Never Happened: The Impact of Enlargement on the Common Foreign and Security Policy Council Working Groups. *European Political Economy Review* (6): 4–30.

Juncos AE and Pomorska K (2008) Does Size Matter? CFSP Committees after Enlargement. *Journal of European Integration* 30(4): 493–509.

Juncos AE and Pomorska K (2011) Invisible and Unaccountable? National Representatives and Council Officials in EU Foreign Policy. *Journal of European Public Policy* 18(8): 1096–1114.

Kassim H, Peters BG, and Wright V (eds) (2000) *The National Co-ordination of EU Policy: The Domestic Level*. Oxford: Oxford University Press.

Kelley J (2009) D-Minus Elections: The Politics and Norms of International Election Observation. *International Organization* 63(4): 765–787.

Kelley J (2010) Election Observers and Their Biases. *Journal of Democracy* 21(3): 158–172.

Khalifa Isaac S (2013) Rethinking the New ENP: A Vision for an Enhanced European Role in the Arab Revolutions. *Democracy and Security* 9(1–2): 40–60.

Klüver H (2012) Informational Lobbying in the European Union: The Effect of Organisational Characteristics. *West European Politics* 35(3): 491–510.

Knill C and Lehmkuhl D (2002) The National Impact of European Union Regulatory Policy: Three Europeanization Mechanisms. *European Journal of Political Research* 41: 255–280.

Kocsis G (2015) EU Election Observation: A Tool for Building Stable Secure Democracies. In: *Security as the Purpose of Law: Conference Papers*. Vilnius: Vilnius University, pp. 100–104.

Koenig N (2011) The EU and the Libyan Crisis: In Quest of Coherence? *The International Spectator* 46(4): 11–30.

Korski D and Gowan R (2009) *Can the EU Rebuild Failing States? A Review of Europe's Civilian Capacities*. London: European Council on Foreign Relations.

Kotyk V (2000) Stručná bilance vývoje české zahraniční politiky. *Mezinárodní vztahy* 35(1): 47–60.

Král D and Bartovic V (2010) *The Czech and Slovak Parliaments after the Lisbon Treaty*. Prague: EUROPEUM Institute for European Policy.

Král D, Bartovic V, and Řiháčková V (2009) *The 2009 Czech EU Presidency: Contested Leadership at a Time of Crisis*. Stockholm: Sieps.

Kronsell A (2002) Can Small States Influence EU Norms? Insights from Sweden's Participation in the Field of Environmental Politics. *Scandinavian Studies* 74(3): 287–304.

Krutílek O (2013) Jak funguje koordinace evropské politiky v ČR? *Euroskop.cz*. Available from: www.euroskop.cz/9047/22346/clanek/jak-funguje-koordinace-evropske-politiky-v-cr.

Ladrech R (2010) *Europeanization and National Politics*. Houndmills: Palgrave Macmillan.

Larsen H (2005) *Analysing the Foreign Policy of Small States in the EU: The Case of Denmark*. Basingstoke: Palgrave Macmillan.

Lempp J (2007) 'COREPER Enlarged': How Enlargement Affected the Functioning of the Committee of Permanent Representatives. *European Political Economy Review* (6): 31–52.

Lenschow A (2006) Europeanisation of Public Policy. In: Richardson J (ed.), *European Union: Power and Policy-Making*. Abingdon: Routledge, pp. 54–70.

Lewis J (2005) The Janus Face of Brussels: Socialization and Everyday Decision Making in the European Union. *International Organization* 59(4): 937–971.

Lewis J (2008) Strategic Bargaining, Norms and Deliberation. In: Naurin D and Wallace H (eds), *Unveiling the Council of the European Union: Games Governments Play in Brussels*. Basingstoke: Palgrave Macmillan, pp. 165–184.

Lidington D (2014) Council Decision Amending Decision 2010/452/CFSP on the European Union Monitoring Mission in Georgia, EUMM GEORGIA. Letter to the Chairman of the House of Lords Select Committee on European Union. Available from: http://europeanmemoranda.cabinetoffice.gov.uk/files/2015/01/Unnumbered_Doc_Decision_2010-452-CFSP_Monitoring_Mission_Georgia_(29237)_Min_Cor_15_December_2014_Lidington-Boswell.pdf.

Lovitt J and Řiháčková V (2008) Is the EU Ready to Put Democracy Assistance at the Heart of European Foreign Policy? *Pasos Policy Brief* (1/2008).

Luif P (2006) *The Austrian EU Presidency: A Midterm Report*. Stockholm: Sieps.

Maass M (2014) Small States: Survival and Proliferation. *International Politics* 51(6): 709–728.

Mahoney C (2008) *Brussels versus the Beltway: Advocacy in the United States and the European Union*. Washington, DC: Georgetown University Press.

Major C (2005) Europeanisation and Foreign and Security Policy: Undermining or Rescuing the Nation State? *Politics* 25(3): 175–190.

Manners I (2002) Normative Power Europe: A Contradiction in Terms? *Journal of Common Market Studies* 40(2): 235–258.

Marek D and Baun M (2010) *The Czech Republic and the European Union*. London: Routledge.

Marks G, Hooghe L, and Blank K (1996) European Integration from the 1980s: State-Centric v. Multi-Level Governance. *Journal of Common Market Studies* 34(3): 341–378.

Mastenbroek E and Kaeding M (2006) Europeanization beyond the Goodness of Fit: Domestic Politics in the Forefront. *Comparative European Politics* 4(4): 331–354.

Mathis JH (2004) Benign Discrimination and the General System of Preferences (GSP). *Legal Issues of Economic Integration* 31(4): 289–303.

Mattila M (2004) Contested Decisions: Empirical Analysis of Voting in the European Union Council of Ministers. *European Journal of Political Research* 43(1): 29–50.

Meerts P (1997) Negotiating in the European Union: Comparing Perceptions of EU Negotiators in Small Member States. *Group Decision and Negotiation* 6(5): 463–482.

Meunier S and Nicolaïdis K (2006) The European Union as a Conflicted Trade Power. *Journal of European Public Policy* 13(6): 906–925.

Meyer-Resende M (2006) *Exporting Legitimacy: The Record of EU Election Observation in the Context of EU Democracy Support*. CEPS Working Document. Available from: www.ceps.eu/system/files/book/1316.pdf.

130 Bibliography

Milward MV (2011) *European Union Electoral Support to Transitional and Non-Established Democracies: The Case of EU's Electoral Observation Missions (1993–2008)*. PhD dissertation, Athens, GA: University of Georgia.

Ministry of Foreign Affairs (2010) *Transition Promotion Concept*. Prague.

Ministry of Foreign Affairs of the Czech Republic (2013) *Souhrnná tabulka projektů realizovaných v roce 2011*. Available from: www.mzv.cz/public/65/35/51/1035238_970240_Tabulka_projektu_2011.xlsx.

Ministry of Foreign Affairs of the Czech Republic (2015a) *Czech Resolution on Participation in Political and Public Affairs Unanimously Adopted*. Available from: www.mzv.cz/mission.geneva/en/human_rights/human_rights_council/czech_resolution_on_participation_in.html.

Ministry of Foreign Affairs of the Czech Republic (2015b) *Odbor společné zahraniční a bezpečnostní politiky EU*. Available from: www.mzv.cz/jnp/cz/o_ministerstvu/organizacni_struktura/utvary_mzv/odbor_spolecne_zahranicni_a_bezpecnostni.html.

Ministry of Foreign Affairs of the Czech Republic (2015c) *Team at the Permanent Representation*. Available from: www.mzv.cz/representation_brussels/en/about_the_representation/team_at_the_permanent_representation/index.html.

Ministry of Industry and Trade of the Czech Republic (2011) *Analýza vlivu změn v seznamu příjemců preferenčního režimu GSP na českou ekonomiku*. Available from: www.socr.cz/file/1675/analyza-vlivu-zmen-v-seznamu-prijemcu-v-gsp-final_1.pdf.

Ministry of Industry and Trade of the Czech Republic (2014) *Teritoriální struktura zahraničního obchodu ČR za leden – červen 2014*. Available from: http://download.mpo.cz/get/37863/58030/614954/priloha001.xlsx.

Ministry of Industry and Trade of the Czech Republic (2015) European Agenda of the Ministry of Industry and Trade of the Czech Republic. Available from: www.mpo.cz/dokument160776.html.

Miskimmon A (2007) *Germany and the Common Foreign and Security Policy of the European Union: Between Europeanisation and National Adaptation*. Basingstoke: Palgrave Macmillan.

Miskimmon A and Paterson WE (2003) Foreign and Security Policy: On the Cusp between Transformation and Accommodation. In: Dyson K and Goetz KH (eds), *Germany, Europe and the Politics of Constraint*. Oxford: Oxford University Press, pp. 325–345.

Moumoutzis K (2011) Still Fashionable yet Useless? Addressing Problems with Research on the Europeanization of Foreign Policy. *Journal of Common Market Studies* 49(3): 607–629.

Najšlová L (2013) Foreign Democracy Assistance in the Czech and Slovak Transitions: What Lessons for the Arab World? *FRIDE Working Paper*. Available from: http://fride.org/download/WP_Democracy_assistance_in_Czech_and_Slovak_Transitions.pdf.

Najšlová L, Řiháčková V, and Shumylo-Tapiola O (2013) The EU in the East: Too Ambitious in Rhetoric, Too Unfocused in Action. In: Fabry E (ed.), *Think Global – Act European IV: Thinking Strategically about the EU's External Action*. Paris: Notre Europe, pp. 225–235.

Nasra S (2011) Governance in EU Foreign Policy: Exploring Small State Influence. *Journal of European Public Policy* 18(2): 164–180.

Němec J and Kuta M (2015) The Character of Membership as a Determinant of Different Performance? An Exploratory Analysis of European Affairs Committees of the Czech Parliament. *Současná Evropa* 20(1): 67–84.

Nielsen KL and Vilson M (2014) The Eastern Partnership: Soft Power Strategy or Policy Failure? *European Foreign Affairs Review* 19(2): 243–262.

Nurmi H and Hosli MO (2003) Which Decision Rule for the Future Council? *European Union Politics* 4(1): 37–50.

Office of the Deputy Prime Minister (2007) *Prioritní oblasti předsednictví České republiky v Radě Evropské unie v prvním pololetí roku 2009*. Available from: www.msmt.cz/uploads/Prioritni_oblasti_CZ_PRES.pdf.

Olsen JP (2002) The Many Faces of Europeanization. *Journal of Common Market Studies* 40(5): 921–952.

OSCE (1999) *Charter for European Security*. Istanbul: OSCE.

OSCE (2010) *Election Observation Handbook*, 6th edn. Warsaw: OSCE/ODIHR.

Ozel I (2013) Differential Europe within a Nation: Europeanization of Regulation across Policy Areas. *Journal of European Public Policy* 20(5): 741–759.

Palosaari T (2011) *The Art of Adaptation: A Study on the Europeanization of Finland's Foreign and Security Policy*. Tampere: Tampere University Press.

Panke D (2010a) Good Instructions in No Time? Domestic Coordination of EU Policies in 19 Small States. *West European Politics* 33(4): 770–790.

Panke D (2010b) *Small States in the European Union: Coping with Structural Disadvantages*. Farnham: Ashgate.

Panke D (2010c) Small States in the European Union: Structural Disadvantages in EU Policy-Making and Counter-Strategies. *Journal of European Public Policy* 17(6): 799–817.

Panke D (2011) Small States in EU Negotiations: Political Dwarfs or Power-Brokers? *Cooperation and Conflict* 46(2): 123–143.

Panke D (2012) Dwarfs in International Negotiations: How Small States Make Their Voices Heard. *Cambridge Review of International Affairs* 25(3): 313–328.

Pedersen T (1998) *Germany, France and the Integration of Europe: A Realist Interpretation*. London: Pinter.

Pedler RH and Schendelen MPCM van (eds) (1994) *Lobbying the European Union: Companies, Trade Associations and Issue Groups*. Aldershot: Dartmouth.

Pijnenburg B (1998) EU Lobbying by Ad Hoc Coalitions: An Exploratory Case Study. *Journal of European Public Policy* 5(2): 303–321.

Placák P (2010) Rozhovor Euroskopu s Alexandrem Vondrou. *Euroskop.cz*, 25 January. Available from: www.euroskop.cz/8801/15189/clanek/rozhovor-euroskopu-s-alexandrem-vondrou.

Pomorska K (2007) The Impact of Enlargement: Europeanization of Polish Foreign Policy? Tracking Adaptation and Change in the Polish Ministry of Foreign Affairs. *The Hague Journal of Diplomacy* 2(1): 25–51.

Přikryl P (2006) Czech Debate on American Missile Defense. *CEPA analysis*. Available from: www.cepa.org/content/czech-debate-american-missile-defense.

Quittkat C and Kotzian P (2011) Lobbying via Consultation: Territorial and Functional Interests in the Commission's Consultation Regime. *Journal of European Integration* 33(4): 401–418.

Radaelli CM (2003) The Europeanization of Public Policy. In: Featherstone K and Radaelli CM (eds), *The Politics of Europeanization*. Oxford: Oxford University Press, pp. 27–56.

Radaelli CM and Dunlop CA (2013) Learning in the European Union: Theoretical Lenses and Meta-Theory. *Journal of European Public Policy* 20(6): 923–940.

Radaelli CM and Pasquier R (2007) Conceptual Issues. In: Graziano P and Vink MP (eds), *Europeanization: New Research Agendas*. Basingstoke: Palgrave Macmillan, pp. 35–45.

Bibliography

Raimundo A (2013) The Europeanisation of Foreign Policy: An Assessment of the EU Impact on Portugal's Post-Colonial Relations in Sub-Saharan Africa. *European Integration Online Papers* 17(1): 1–23.

Reinhard J (2012) 'Because We Are All Europeans!' When Do EU Member States Use Normative Arguments? *Journal of European Public Policy* 19(9): 1336–1356.

Reynaert V (2012) The European Union's Foreign Policy since the Treaty of Lisbon: The Difficult Quest for More Consistency and Coherence. *The Hague Journal of Diplomacy* 7(2): 207–226.

Rickli J-M (2008) European Small States' Military Policies after the Cold War: From Territorial to Niche Strategies. *Cambridge Review of International Affairs* 21(3): 307–325.

Řiháčková V and von Seydlitz C (2007) Václav Klaus and the Constitutional Treaty: Czech Euroscepsis or Eurorealism? *EUROPEUM Position Paper*. Available from: http://pdc.ceu.hu/archive/00003159/01/vaclav_klaus_constitutional_treaty.pdf.

Risse T (2000) 'Let's Argue!': Communicative Action in World Politics. *International Organization* 54(1): 1–39.

Risse T, Cowles MG, and Caporaso J (2001) Europeanization and Domestic Change: Introduction. In: Cowles MG, Caporaso J, and Risse T (eds), *Transforming Europe: Europeanization and Domestic Change*. Ithaca, NY and London: Cornell University Press, pp. 1–20.

Romsloe BO (2004) EU's External Policy: Are the Lilliputians Impotent or Potent? The Case of Crisis Management in the Amsterdam Treaty. *ARENA Working Papers* 23: 1–30.

Rubešková M, Schulzová H, and Weiss T (2014) *Racionalizace sítě zastupitelských úřadů*, EUROPEUM Research Paper. Praha: Institut pro evropskou politiku EUROPEUM. Available from: www.europeum.org/data/articles/racionalizace-zastoupeni.pdf.

Sartori G (1970) Concept Misinformation in Comparative Politics. *American Political Science Review* 64: 1033–1053.

Saurugger S (2013) Constructivism and Public Policy Approaches in the EU: From Ideas to Power Games. *Journal of European Public Policy* 20(6): 888–906.

Schimmelfennig F and Sedelmeier U (2007) Candidate Countries and Conditionality. In: Graziano P and Vink MP (eds), *Europeanization: New Research Agendas*. Basingstoke: Palgrave Macmillan, pp. 88–101.

Sedláček M (2010) Evropeizace soukromého sektoru na příkladu českého pivovarnictví. *Politologický časopis* 17(2): 183–211.

Selck TJ (2006) *Preferences and Procedures: European Union Legislative Decision-Making*. Dordrecht: Springer.

Šepták M (2009) Místo Rakouska v české (československé) zahraniční politice. In: Kořan M (ed.), *Česká zahraniční politika v zrcadle sociálně-vědního výzkumu*. Praha: Ústav mezinárodních vztahů, pp. 44–71.

Shaffer G and Apea Y (2005) Institutional Choice in the Generalized System of Preferences Case: Who Decides the Conditions for Trade Preferences? The Law and Politics of Rights. *Journal of World Trade* 39(6): 977–1008.

Siles-Brügge G (2014) EU Trade and Development Policy beyond the ACP: Subordinating Developmental to Commercial Imperatives in the Reform of GSP. *Contemporary Politics* 20(1): 49–62.

Sjursen H (2011) Not So Intergovernmental after All? On Democracy and Integration in European Foreign and Security Policy. *Journal of European Public Policy* 18(8): 1078–1095.

Sládeček V, Mikule V, and Syllová J (2007) *Ústava České republiky: komentář*. Praha: C.H. Beck.
Šlosarčík I (2006) Europeizace české veřejné správy: česká cesta, evropské prošlapané chodníčky nebo evropská administrativní magistrála? *Pražské sociálně vědní studie – Teritoriální řada* (TER-018): 3–26.
Smith KE (2007) The Role of Democracy Assistance in Future EU External Relations. In: van Doorn M and von Meijenfeldt R (eds), *Democracy, Europe's Core Value? On the European Profile in World-Wide Democracy Assistance*. Delft: Eburon, pp. 129–137.
Smith M (2004) Toward a Theory of EU Foreign Policy-Making: Multi-Level Governance, Domestic Politics, and National Adaptation to Europe's Common Foreign and Security Policy. *Journal of European Public Policy* 11(4): 740–758.
Smith ME (2004) Institutionalization, Policy Adaptation and European Foreign Policy Cooperation. *European Journal of International Relations* 10(1): 95–136.
Smith ME (2011) Implementation: Making the EU's International Relations Work. In: Hill C and Smith M (eds), *International Relations and the European Union*. Oxford: Oxford University Press, pp. 171–193.
Souček M (2011) Koordinace evropských záležitostí v České republice. In: Hokovský R and Lebeda V (eds), *Tajemství českého úspěchu v EU?!*. Praha: Konrad-Adenauer-Stiftung and Evropské hodnoty, pp. 191–216.
Steinmetz R and Wivel A (eds) (2010) *Small States in Europe: Challenges and Opportunities*. Farnham: Ashgate.
Stetter S (2004) Cross-Pillar Politics: Functional Unity and Institutional Fragmentation of EU Foreign Policies. *Journal of European Public Policy* 11(4): 720–739.
Stewart E (2008) Capabilities and Coherence? The Evolution of European Union Conflict Prevention. *European Foreign Affairs Review* 13(2): 229–253.
Stone Sweet A and Sandholtz W (1998) Integration, Supranational Governance, and the Institutionalization of the European Polity. In: Sandholtz W and Stone Sweet A (eds), *European Integration and Supranational Governance*. Oxford: Oxford University Press, pp. 1–26.
Stone Sweet A, Fligstein N, and Sandholtz W (2001) The Institutionalization of European Space. In: Stone Sweet A, Sandholtz W, and Fligstein N (eds), *The Institutionalization of Europe*. Oxford: Oxford University Press, pp. 1–28.
Tallberg J (2008) Bargaining Power in the European Council. *Journal of Common Market Studies* 46(3): 685–708.
Teti A, Thompson D, and Noble C (2013) EU Democracy Assistance Discourse in Its New Response to a Changing Neighbourhood. *Democracy and Security* 9(1–2): 61–79.
Thomson R (2011) *Resolving Controversy in European Union: Legislative Decision-Making before and after Enlargement*. Cambridge: Cambridge University Press.
Thorhallsson B and Wivel A (2006) Small States in the European Union: What Do We Know and What Would We Like to Know? *Cambridge Review of International Affairs* 19(4): 651–668.
Tocci N (2011) *The European Union and the Arab Spring: A (Missed?) Opportunity to Revamp the European Neighbourhood Policy*. EuroMesco Brief. Available from: www.euromesco.net/images/iemedeuromescobrief2.pdf.
Tomuschat C (2008) *Human Rights: Between Idealism and Realism*. Oxford: Oxford University Press.
Törő C, Butler E, and Grúber K (2014) Visegrád: The Evolving Pattern of Coordination and Partnership after EU Enlargement. *Europe–Asia Studies* 66(3): 364–393.

Torreblanca JI (2001) Ideas, Preferences and Institutions: Explaining the Europeanization of Spanish Foreign Policy. *ARENA Working Papers*, no. WP 01/26.

Treib O and Falkner G (2009) Bargaining and Lobbying in EU Social Policy. In: Coen D and Richardson J (eds), *Lobbying the European Union: Institutions, Actors, and Issues*. Oxford: Oxford University Press, pp. 256–276.

Tulmets E (2009) Revisiting Europeanisation: The Role of Social Actors in the EU Accession Process. In: Devaux S and Sudbery I (eds), *Europeanisation: Social Actors and the Transfer of Models in EU-27*. Prague: CEFRES, pp. 25–55.

UNCTAD (2008) *Generalized System of Preferences: Handbook on the Scheme of the European Community*. New York and Geneva: United Nations.

United Nations (2005) Declaration of Principles for International Election Observation and Code of Conduct for International Election Observers.

Vajdová T (2003) Limits of Public Debate in the EU Pre-Accession Period: Czech Republic. In: Gorman S (ed.), *Locations of the Political*. Vienna: IWM.

van Keulen M (2006) *Going Europe or Going Dutch: How the Dutch Government Shapes European Union Policy*. Amsterdam: Amsterdam University Press.

van Schendelen R (2010) *More Machiavelli in Brussels: The Art of Lobbying the EU*. Amsterdam: Amsterdam University Press.

Veen T (2011) *The Political Economy of Collective Decision-Making: Conflicts and Coalitions in the Council of the European Union*. Berlin and Heidelberg: Springer-Verlag.

Vink MP and Graziano P (2007) Challenges of a New Research Agenda. In: Graziano P and Vink MP (eds), *Europeanization: New Research Agendas*. Basingstoke: Palgrave Macmillan, pp. 3–20.

Waer P and Driessen B (1995) The New European Union Generalised System of Preferences. *Journal of World Trade* 29(4): 97.

Wallace H (2005) Exercising Power and Influence in the European Union: The Roles of Member States. In: Bulmer S and Lequesne C (eds), *The Member States of the European Union*. Oxford: Oxford University Press, pp. 25–44.

Watts D (2007) *Pressure Groups*. Edinburgh: Edinburgh University Press.

Weiss T (2011) Projecting the Re-Discovered: Czech Policy towards Eastern Europe. *Perspectives: Review of International Affairs* 19(2): 27–44.

Weiss T (2015a) Building Leverage at the EU level? Specialisation and Coherence in Czech Policy on Eastern European Transition. *Journal of International Relations and Development* [advanced online publication 14 August 2015]. doi: 10.1057/jird.2015.29.

Weiss T (2015b) Confused and Divided: Czech Foreign and Security Policy in the EU. In: Fiott D (ed.), *The Common Security and Defence Policy: National Perspectives*. Gent: Academia Press, pp. 87–88.

Weiss T (2016) Too Limited, Too Late: Evaluating the Czech Republic's Performance as a Small-State Lobbyist in EU External Policy. *New Perspectives* 24(1): 53–78.

Weiss T, Mikhelidze N, and Šlosarčík I (2013) Multilateralism as Envisaged? Assessing European Union's Engagement in Conflict Resolution in the Neighbourhood. In: Bouchard C, Peterson J, and Tocci N (eds), *Multilateralism in the 21st Century: Europe's Quest for Effectiveness*. London and New York: Routledge, pp. 157–177.

Wessels W, Maurer A, and Mittag J (eds) (2003) *Fifteen into One? The European Union and Its Member States*. Manchester and New York: Manchester University Press.

Wetzel A and Orbie J (2012) *The EU's Promotion of External Democracy: In Search of the Plot*. CEPS Policy Brief. Available from: http://aei.pitt.edu/36821/1/ceps_9.pdf.

White B (2001) *Understanding European Foreign Policy*. Houndmills: Palgrave.

Wivel A (2005) The Security Challenge of Small EU Member States: Interests, Identity and the Development of the EU as a Security Actor. *Journal of Common Market Studies* 43(2): 393–412.

Wivel A, Bailes AJK, and Archer C (2014) Setting the Scene: Small States and International Security. In: Archer C, Bailes AJK, and Wivel A (eds), *Small States and International Security: Europe and Beyond*. Abingdon: Routledge, pp. 3–25.

Wolczuk K (2009) Implementation without Coordination: The Impact of EU Conditionality on Ukraine under the European Neighbourhood Policy. *Europe-Asia Studies* 61(2): 187–211.

Wong RY (2006) *The Europeanization of French Foreign Policy; France and the EU in East Asia*. Basingstoke: Palgrave Macmillan.

Wong R and Hill C (eds) (2011) *National and European Foreign Policies: Towards Europeanization*. London and New York: Routledge.

Young AR and Peterson J (2014) *Parochial Global Europe: 21st Century Trade Politics*. Oxford: Oxford University Press.

Youngs R (2001) European Union Democracy Promotion Policies: Ten Years on. *European Foreign Affairs Review* 6(3): 355–373.

Zemanová Š (2008) *Evropeizace zahraniční politiky v oblasti lidských práv*. Praha: Oeconomica.

Zetter L (2011) *Lobbying: The Art of Political Persuasion*. Petersfield: Harriman House.

Zubek R (2008) *Core Executive and Europeanization in Central Europe*. Basingstoke: Palgrave Macmillan.

Index

Abkhazia 98–9, 102
Accession Treaty 20, 60
advocacy *see* lobbying
African Union 86
agenda-setting 10, 12, 70, 97
aid: predictability of 77; *see also* official development assistance
alliance 10, 23, 105, 111
aluminium 67
annexation 100, 106
Antici group 34–5, 41
Arab Spring 74, 77, 80–1, 83
Argentina 69
Article 133 Committee *see* Trade Policy Committee
Ashton, Catherine 81
Association for Democracy Assistance and Human Rights 81
Austria 78

Balkans, the 78
Baltic states 102–3
Barcelona Process *see* Euro-Mediterranean Partnership
behaviour 1, 4, 7, 13, 18, 57, 85, 107, 110, 112, 114–15
Belarus 91
Ben Ali, Zine el-Abidine 74
Bouazizi, Mohamed 74
Brazil 69
Brusselization 112; *see also* Europeanization
budget 16, 74, 76, 78, 84–5, 87–9, 91–7, 100
business 10, 27, 30–2, 36, 38, 45, 50–1, 53–4, 69, 71, 80, 101, 104, 115

cabinet 36, 38, 45, 49–54, 82–3
capability 5, 97–8, 100–1
capacity 4, 12, 49, 70, 77
CARIFORUM 64
Central African Republic 97
Central Europe 23, 74, 76, 101, 115
Chad 97
Civic Democratic Party 67
Civilian Planning and Conduct Capability 98
civil society 22, 65, 74–5, 79, 90
Club Med 81
COHOM *see* Human Rights Working Group
Committee for Civilian Aspects of Crisis Management 34–5, 41, 61, 97–8, 100–4
Committee of Permanent Representatives 27, 34–5, 41, 61, 66, 78–9, 82
Common Security and Defence Policy 7, 12, 16–18, 23–4, 29–30, 34, 41–3, 46–7, 56–7, 59, 84, 97–8, 100–1, 103–4, 106, 108, 110–11
Commonwealth 86
communication 7–8, 27, 29–31, 64, 95
comprehensive approach 98, 100, 105
conditionality 77, 81–3
confidence-building 98–100, 103–5
constructivism 2–3, 112
coordination: of lobbying activities 12, 22; of national policy 12, 14–15, 18, 20, 22, 24–31, 86, 101, 115
Crimea 100, 106
crisis management 9, 70, 78, 97–8, 101–2

Crisis Management and Planning Directorate 98–100
Cuba 91
Czech Forum for Development Cooperation 81
Czech Republic: as a case study 15; as accession country 20–1; competence law of 25; domestic debate in 21; foreign policy of 22–4; parliament of 21–2, 25, 27–8, 32, 57, 101; president of 21, 25–6, 90

defence 6, 12, 16–18, 21, 23, 29, 33–4, 96, 99–101, 103, 105, 108
democracy 13, 16–18, 22–4, 34, 41–3, 46–7, 55–7, 59–61, 75–80, 82, 85, 87–8, 90–2, 94–5, 108–10, 113–15
Democratic Republic of Congo 4
Denmark 65, 69, 100
Department for Human Rights and Transition Promotion 79, 90, 94
Development Cooperation Instrument 85
dissidents 23, 79, 90

early warning 9, 14–15, 32, 47, 58–9, 108, 112, 115; methods to acquire 45; significance of 11
Eastern Europe 24, 48, 73–4, 76, 79–80, 82, 102, 109–10
Eastern Partnership 74, 79, 83–4
Eastern Partnership Civil Society Forum 91
Egypt 84
Election Observation and Democratic Support 86, 88
enlargement 2, 12, 24, 29, 73–4, 78–9
EU Military Committee 61, 101
Euro-Mediterranean Partnership 73
European External Action Service 4, 8, 12, 16, 27, 35, 38–9, 45, 49–56, 77–8, 80, 84, 86, 88–9, 93, 97–8, 100, 102–5
European Commission 2, 4, 10, 12, 16, 19, 27, 32, 35–6, 38–9, 45–6, 49–56, 59, 63–5, 67–8, 70–1, 73–8, 80–90, 93, 95–6, 98–100, 103, 105, 115
European Community 6, 62, 85

European Council 2, 3, 25, 27, 100, 103, 105
European Council on Foreign Relations 101
European Initiative for Democracy and Human Rights 85; *see also* European Instrument for Democracy and Human Rights
European Instrument for Democracy and Human Rights 17, 85, 87–96
Europeanization 1, 4–7, 13, 21, 107–8, 112, 114
European Neighbourhood and Partnership Instrument 75–6, 78
European Neighbourhood Instrument 73, 76, 85; *fourchette* in 77–8, 80, 82–3
European Neighbourhood Policy 12, 16–8, 24, 29, 34, 41–3, 46–9, 56–7, 59–60, 73–84, 108–12; revision of 74–5
European Parliament 4, 12, 16, 31, 39, 46, 55–7, 64–6, 69, 71–2, 78, 82–3, 86, 88–90, 93–6, 115; Committee on International Trade of 64–5, 69; Committee on Development of 64; members of 20, 33, 36, 38, 45, 50–4, 65–6, 69–70, 72, 90
European Union Committee 26–31, 80
Eurorealism 21, 33
"Everything but Arms" 63
excellence 20, 114
experience 3, 9, 13–14, 30, 41–3, 58–60, 73, 79, 91, 102, 108, 110–11, 113
expertise 3–4, 9, 11–12, 20, 27, 37–9, 45, 50–1, 53–8, 80–1, 87, 92, 94–5, 101–2, 109, 111, 113

ferro-chromium 67
freedom: of speech 91; media 79, 91
framework position 27–9, 31–2
France 24, 76, 81, 83, 97
frozen conflict 103
Füle, Štefan 81

Generalised System of Preferences 17, 62–72; graduation from 63, 72; history of 62; number of beneficiaries 63; GSP+ 63, 65, 67

Georgia 17, 97–105, 111
Germany 65, 69, 78, 81, 83, 102, 105, 111

Havel, Václav 90
Heads of Missions 32, 83, 90, 98
High Representative of the Union for Foreign Affairs and Security Policy 36, 38, 45, 50–1, 54, 75, 81, 87, 98
human capital 60
Human Development Index 68
human resources 57, 61, 113–15; *see also* human capital
human rights: defenders of 79, 90; generations of 76
Human Rights Council of the United Nations 91
Human Rights Working Group 34–5, 41, 60–1, 89, 91, 93–4, 96, 113
Hungary 103, 114–15

image 1, 21, 39, 55–6, 104
impartiality 70
Incident Prevention and Reporting Mechanism 99
individuals 10, 12, 17, 20, 28, 41, 43, 57–8, 61, 91, 113; role of 31–2, 58, 110–11
Instrument for Pre-accession Assistance 85
intergovernmentality 2–3, 16, 18, 103, 111
internal market 16, 23–4, 29, 66–7, 116
International Labour Organization 63
insider status 14–5, 32, 44, 46–7, 58–9, 95, 109, 112–15; methods to acquire 11, 45, 109; significance of 10–11
institution-building 75, 98
Israel 79
Italy 103

Kazakhstan 67–9, 71
Klaus, Václav 21
knowledge 3, 7, 9–11, 14–15, 20–1, 40, 78, 85, 91, 94, 101, 112–13
Kosovo 101, 104, 106
Kukan, Eduard 82

Latin America 24, 31, 69, 86
leadership 67, 81, 105, 111

learning 6, 13–15, 19–20, 43, 46–7, 57–8, 95, 107–10, 113–14, 116
least developed countries 63
Lisbon Treaty 8, 64, 79, 98
lobbying 4, 7–13, 18, 36, 38, 45, 49–54, 70, 81, 115; literature on 1–2, 8, 18, 44, 55, 58, 94, 107–9, 112, 115–16; role of 9; strategies of 8, 11, 58

Mali 84, 97, 101
management 95, 97, 102, 106, 115
mandate 27–8, 83, 97–102, 104–5
methanol 67
Middle East 24, 48, 79
Ministry of Agriculture 30
Ministry of Defence 101
Ministry of Interior 101
Moldova 82
monitoring 86, 98–9, 101, 105
more-for-more principle 17, 71, 75–8, 80–4, 111
motivation 8, 63, 74, 81, 83, 87, 98, 102, 112
multiannual financial framework 76, 87–9, 91, 96

national interest 3, 5, 7, 13–16, 22, 34, 41, 45, 49, 55–7, 59, 111–12, 114
Netherlands, the 65, 69, 100, 103, 114
new member states 6, 15, 20, 107, 114
Nicolaidis group 34–5, 41
non-governmental organizations 11, 24, 28, 36, 38, 45, 50–1, 53–4, 80–1, 86, 88, 90, 94–6, 109
non-paper 35, 38, 45, 49–51, 53–4, 69, 71, 100, 103
non-state actors 17, 28–9, 36, 38, 45, 50–1, 53–4, 115
North Atlantic Treaty Organization 16, 21–4, 30, 33, 78, 100–1

Obama, Barack 101
Office for Democratic Institutions and Human Rights 86, 91
official development assistance 67–8
opt-out 100
ordinary legislative procedure 16, 64–5, 88

Organisation for Economic Co-operation and Development 23
Organization for Security and Co-operation in Europe 22, 86, 91, 99
Organization of American States 86

performance 15, 40–1, 47, 56–9, 71–2, 77, 84, 88, 94–5, 110–12, 114–15
permanent representation 27, 29–34, 39, 41–2, 55–8, 60–1, 69, 71–2, 79, 92, 103, 108, 111, 116
Poland 6, 65, 76, 79, 81, 83, 102–3, 105, 111, 115
polarization 89, 100, 103, 106, 114–15
policy cycle 10, 46, 67, 70–1
Political and Security Committee 31–2, 34–5, 41, 79, 89, 92–5, 97–8, 101, 103–4
political dialogue 90
political party 33, 67, 115
politicization 21, 114–15
Portugal 64
post-Soviet countries 79
power: normative 85; market 62; trade 62
presidency 3–4, 15, 35, 38, 45, 49–54, 59, 65, 69–70, 97; Czech Council 15, 20, 25–7, 61, 79, 83, 91, 101
Project Cell 100, 104

qualified majority voting 2, 41, 64–5, 88, 110

rapporteur 64, 82
rational choice 1–2, 112
rule of law 23, 76, 79, 98
Russia 67–9, 71–2, 86, 98–100, 102, 106

salience 8, 16, 47–8, 59, 110, 112, 116
Schwarzenberg, Karel 80
Sectorial Coordination Group 26–31, 33
Sierra Leone 91, 93, 96
silent procedure 27, 29
size 22, 34, 49, 62, 77, 82, 87–9, 96–100, 102, 116; as negotiation factor 3, 38–9, 52, 55–6, 60, 111; definition of 18

skills 11, 101, 110
Slovakia 82, 96, 103
socialization 3, 13, 110, 112–13
Southern Mediterranean 73, 75, 79, 84
South Korea 64
South Ossetia 98–9, 102
Spain 30, 65, 69
special envoy 79, 84
specialization 4, 12, 37–9, 45, 50–1, 53–4, 59, 109, 113
special representative 99
stabilization 98–9
stakeholders 9, 11–12, 16–17, 44, 70–1, 104, 109–10
strategic review 17, 98–100, 102–4
success 3–4, 10–12, 14–15, 22–3, 38–9, 55–6, 58, 60, 62–3, 65, 71–2, 82, 94–5, 99, 107–8, 110, 114, 116
Sweden 76, 79, 102–3, 111, 114

tactics 1, 10, 31, 111–12
Trade Policy Committee 32, 34–5, 41, 61, 64, 66, 72
transformation *see* transition
transition 22, 67, 69, 75, 79–81, 84, 90–5
Transparency International 11
Treaty on European Union 85
Tunisia 74

Ukraine 72, 82, 91, 100, 103
unanimity 2–3, 6, 16, 59, 97, 103, 111
Union for Mediterranean 74, 79
United Kingdom 24, 65, 69–70, 81–2, 83, 97, 111
United Nations 23, 63, 86, 91–2, 94, 99
United States of America 21, 64, 78, 100

veto 3, 6, 8, 99
Visegrád Group 82, 103, 112

Weimar Group 103
World Trade Organization 23, 62–3, 68
World Bank 63, 68

Taylor & Francis eBooks

Helping you to choose the right eBooks for your Library

Add Routledge titles to your library's digital collection today. Taylor and Francis ebooks contains over 50,000 titles in the Humanities, Social Sciences, Behavioural Sciences, Built Environment and Law.

Choose from a range of subject packages or create your own!

Benefits for you
- Free MARC records
- COUNTER-compliant usage statistics
- Flexible purchase and pricing options
- All titles DRM-free.

Benefits for your user
- Off-site, anytime access via Athens or referring URL
- Print or copy pages or chapters
- Full content search
- Bookmark, highlight and annotate text
- Access to thousands of pages of quality research at the click of a button.

REQUEST YOUR FREE INSTITUTIONAL TRIAL TODAY
Free Trials Available
We offer free trials to qualifying academic, corporate and government customers.

eCollections – Choose from over 30 subject eCollections, including:

Archaeology	Language Learning
Architecture	Law
Asian Studies	Literature
Business & Management	Media & Communication
Classical Studies	Middle East Studies
Construction	Music
Creative & Media Arts	Philosophy
Criminology & Criminal Justice	Planning
Economics	Politics
Education	Psychology & Mental Health
Energy	Religion
Engineering	Security
English Language & Linguistics	Social Work
Environment & Sustainability	Sociology
Geography	Sport
Health Studies	Theatre & Performance
History	Tourism, Hospitality & Events

For more information, pricing enquiries or to order a free trial, please contact your local sales team:
www.tandfebooks.com/page/sales

Routledge
Taylor & Francis Group

The home of Routledge books

www.tandfebooks.com